8 Handy Frozen Veg

Peas   ☐ ☐ ☐ ☐ ☐
Sweetcorn   ☐ ☐ ☐ ☐ ☐
Spinach   ☐ ☐ ☐ ☐ ☐
Edamame Beans   ☐ ☐ ☐ ☐ ☐
Broad Beans   ☐ ☐ ☐ ☐ ☐
....   ☐ ☐ ☐ ☐ ☐

9 Cucurbits & Aubergines

Cucumber   ☐ ☐ ☐ ☐ ☐
Courgettes   ☐ ☐ ☐ ☐ ☐
Pumpkin and Squash   ☐ ☐ ☐ ☐ ☐
Aubergines   ☐ ☐ ☐ ☐ ☐
....   ☐ ☐ ☐ ☐ ☐

10 Tomatoes

Fresh   ☐ ☐ ☐ ☐ ☐
Tinned   ☐ ☐ ☐ ☐ ☐
Passata   ☐ ☐ ☐ ☐ ☐
Sun-dried   ☐ ☐ ☐ ☐ ☐

11 Avocados

Avocado!   ☐ ☐ ☐ ☐ ☐

12 Peppers and Chillies

Green/Red/Yellow Peppers   ☐ ☐ ☐ ☐ ☐
Romano (long) Peppers   ☐ ☐ ☐ ☐ ☐
Chillies (red and green)   ☐ ☐ ☐ ☐ ☐
....   ☐ ☐ ☐ ☐ ☐

13 Mushrooms

Flat   ☐ ☐ ☐ ☐ ☐
Button   ☐ ☐ ☐ ☐ ☐
Chestnut   ☐ ☐ ☐ ☐ ☐
Portobello   ☐ ☐ ☐ ☐ ☐
Oyster   ☐ ☐ ☐ ☐ ☐
Shiitake   ☐ ☐ ☐ ☐ ☐
King Oyster   ☐ ☐ ☐ ☐ ☐
Wild Mushrooms   ☐ ☐ ☐ ☐ ☐
Dried Porcini   ☐ ☐ ☐ ☐ ☐
....   ☐ ☐ ☐ ☐ ☐

14 Preserv...

(in vinegar or...)

Olives   ☐ ☐ ☐ ☐ ☐
Capers   ☐ ☐ ☐ ☐ ☐
Gherkins   ☐ ☐ ☐ ☐ ☐
Pickled Onions   ☐ ☐ ☐ ☐ ☐
Pickled Beetroot   ☐ ☐ ☐ ☐ ☐
Artichoke Hearts   ☐ ☐ ☐ ☐ ☐
....   ☐ ☐ ☐ ☐ ☐
....   ☐ ☐ ☐ ☐ ☐

15 Leafy, Salady Herbs

Parsley   ☐ ☐ ☐ ☐ ☐
Mint   ☐ ☐ ☐ ☐ ☐
Chives   ☐ ☐ ☐ ☐ ☐
Coriander   ☐ ☐ ☐ ☐ ☐
Basil   ☐ ☐ ☐ ☐ ☐
Rocket   ☐ ☐ ☐ ☐ ☐
Nasturtiums (leaves/flowers)   ☐ ☐ ☐ ☐ ☐
Dill   ☐ ☐ ☐ ☐ ☐
Tarragon   ☐ ☐ ☐ ☐ ☐
....   ☐ ☐ ☐ ☐ ☐
....   ☐ ☐ ☐ ☐ ☐

16 Pungent Herbs

Rosemary   ☐ ☐ ☐ ☐ ☐
Thyme   ☐ ☐ ☐ ☐ ☐
Bay leaves   ☐ ☐ ☐ ☐ ☐
Oregano/Marjoram   ☐ ☐ ☐ ☐ ☐
Sage   ☐ ☐ ☐ ☐ ☐
....   ☐ ☐ ☐ ☐ ☐

17 Seaweeds & Shore Veg

Nori Sheets   ☐ ☐ ☐ ☐ ☐
Sea Lettuce   ☐ ☐ ☐ ☐ ☐
Dulse   ☐ ☐ ☐ ☐ ☐
Kelp   ☐ ☐ ☐ ☐ ☐
Seaweed   ☐ ☐ ☐ ☐ ☐
Samphire   ☐ ☐ ☐ ☐ ☐
....   ☐ ☐ ☐ ☐ ☐

How to Eat 30 Plants a Week

How to Eat 30 Plants a Week

Hugh Fearnley-Whittingstall

Introduction by Tim Spector

Photography by Lizzie Mayson

BLOOMSBURY PUBLISHING
LONDON • OXFORD • NEW YORK • NEW DELHI • SYDNEY

*For Mum and Dad, who have never
stinted on the plants*

Using the recipes

- This book is intended to be useful for omnivores, vegetarians and vegans, helping you all to eat at least 30 plants a week. With this in mind, outside of the Meat and Fish chapters, and with the exception of a few suggested swaps and additions, all the recipes are veggie, and most of them are easily adapted to be vegan.

- All spoon measures are level unless otherwise stated: 1 tsp = 5ml spoon; 1 tbsp = 15ml spoon.

- All herbs are fresh unless otherwise suggested.

- Use freshly ground black pepper unless otherwise listed.

- Where 'a little oil or fat for cooking' is suggested my preference is for ghee or coconut oil, but you can use another vegetable oil, such as sunflower or groundnut. Avoid using extra virgin or cold-pressed oils for frying, especially extra virgin olive oil.

- All fruit and vegetables should be washed before you start cooking. Please choose organic fruit and veg if you can.

- Please choose unwaxed/organic citrus fruit as I suggest using the zest in many recipes.

- Onions and garlic are peeled unless otherwise suggested. Peeling fresh ginger and turmeric is optional, I usually don't.

- Root vegetables can be peeled, or simply scrubbed, according to their condition, and your preference.

- Please use free-range eggs, preferably organic.

- Timings are provided for conventional and fan-assisted ovens. As ovens vary, these are intended as guidelines, with a description of the desired final colour or texture of the dish as a further guide.

Contents

Introduction

by Tim Spector

This book is timely and exciting: it captures a converging view among leading nutritionists, that eating around 30 different plants a week is really beneficial to our health. I've been communicating this idea for a while now in the context of my research and I've seen that it's been a hugely successful message; it's such a simple idea that resonates with so many people, and has helped me improve the variety of plants I eat myself.

I know from spending time with Hugh in the kitchen that the idea has inspired him too, and this lovely collection of richly varied, plant-laden recipes is the result. He's asked me to explain here the reasons *why* it's such a good idea to implement the 30 plants approach into daily life. It's my pleasure to do so, because the science behind the concept is truly fascinating.

Eating a greater variety of plants in order to improve our health is not new science. There are countless studies and large reviews that confirm the positive effects that eating fruits and vegetables, pulses and legumes, whole grains, nuts and seeds, herbs and spices has on our health. There has also been plenty of research that shows eating more than the much-vaunted 'five a day' is even better for us, decreasing the risk of illness and improving outcomes for brain function, nutrient status, gut health and more.

Until fairly recently, these plant foods were thought to be so beneficial mainly because of their micro-nutrient content, with particular focus on vitamins. Vitamins E and C in particular got lots of attention and there are some very successful commercial supplements available as a result. However, their success is not backed by any science. If anything, very high doses of these individual vitamins in supplement form can do more harm than good. On the other hand, eating a variety of plants that contain these vitamins (and much else that is good for us besides) is a far better approach.

Many scientists focused on the powerful effects of individual chemicals found in plants, known as phytochemicals – such as sulforaphane in broccoli or beta-carotene in, unsurprisingly, carrots. While these specific plant chemicals do have a powerful effect and play an important role as 'reactive oxygen species scavengers', mopping up pro-inflammatory chemicals, they aren't the sole drivers of the wonderfully complex and persistent impact that plants have on our health. This is because plants like this contain *thousands* of different chemicals of potential benefit, not just the 'stars' we talk about.

We are now beginning to understand that it is the complex *combinations and interactions* of fibres, phytochemicals and plant proteins that makes plants so unique. Our digestive system has evolved with our gut microbes precisely to give them the space (large surface area of the gut) and time (longer length of the gut compared to other mammals) to break down and use all the different components effectively. We can't do this ourselves because we don't make the enzymes necessary to break down plant fibres and transform phytochemicals, and so we need our gut microbes. These are technically speaking separate from 'us', in the sense that we don't 'make' them. They have just come to stay – and they have evolved to do some vital jobs for us while in residence. They are able to do the tasks we can't because they have 500 times more genes than we do, and are incredibly versatile at interacting with the food we eat.

The way in which our gut physiology has evolved to accommodate our gut microbes shows just how important plants have always been in our diet. Our gut microbes thrive on having a variety of fibres to choose from, using each of them to make different chemicals for us like mini personal pharmacies. Even the synthesis of the major neurotransmitters, like dopamine, oxytocin and adrenaline, are facilitated by healthy gut microbes.

Many microbes appear to be fussy and have favourite foods, with specific strains increasing rapidly in response when we eat that food. A great example we discovered recently in our research with ZOE (the personal nutrition programme that I co-founded) is a finicky microbe, *Lawsonibacter*, that only grows if you feed it coffee. It has possible health benefits that people who drink only tea may not enjoy (that's not to say tea drinkers don't benefit from other plants in other ways!).

The other reason to eat a variety of plants is to get a wide range of polyphenol chemicals. These are a group of thousands of chemicals that plants use to defend themselves in various ways, often against parasites or predators. As part of their functionality, they also give colour, taste, tannins and some bitterness. Many of them provide the energy and chemical diversity our microbes need to work properly. So, a purple carrot will have different polyphenols to an orange carrot, a red pepper different to a green one, etc.

Just as good microbes will increase with a high plant diet rich in omega-3 fatty acids, for which many nuts and seeds are an excellent source (as well as oily fish like mackerel and salmon), bad microbes will feast on unhealthy foods (especially ultra processed foods) to make inflammatory chemicals. This is why it's so important to focus on plants first. By adding a rich variety of plants to our diets, we are welcoming in as many of the good guys as possible, and crowding out the baddies at the same time.

My research with the combined American and British Gut Project explored the relationship between diet and a helpful gut biome in more detail (journals.asm.org/doi/10.1128/ msystems.00031-18). Looking at a subgroup of the 11,000 community science volunteers who completed a food frequency questionnaire and gut microbe analysis, we were surprised to discover that it wasn't dietary patterns such as 'vegan', 'omnivore' or 'vegetarian' that had the biggest impact on microbiome health. It was the variety of different plants people ate that gave rise to the most positive outcomes.

It began to emerge that around 30 plants seemed optimal, both in the sense that the health benefits for eating higher numbers than 30 started to plateau, and also because a significant number of participants were managing to get to 30, or pretty close. We then compared those who reported eating 30-plus different plants per week with those who reported eating 10 or fewer. By comparing the two extremes of the plant consumption scale, we worked out how much difference this increase in plant diversity made.

The over-30-plant-eaters had on average a much greater diversity of gut microbes (meaning more species) than the low plant group. High diversity is consistently linked to reduced risk of common diseases, from obesity and diabetes to dementia, depression and heart disease, to autoimmune diseases and allergies. They were also more likely to have bacterial strains that ferment fibre to make helpful short-chain fatty acid chemicals that are great for the immune system.

Unexpectedly, those who ate 30 or more plants were less likely to have genes for antibiotic resistance, putting them on the right side of what is becoming a huge issue for public health. We know that excess antibiotics used in producing meat contribute to antimicrobial resistance and eating more plants reduces this exposure. Plants also contain polyphenol chemicals that via gut microbes give us a strengthened immune system, making us less susceptible to infections that require antibiotic treatment. Either way, eating more plants helps the fight against antimicrobial resistance. Though this is just one study, other cohort studies from Belgium and the Netherlands, as well as our UK study of 14,000 twins, have found that eating more fibre and plants is strongly correlated with good gut microbe health.

And so the message of *30 Plants a Week* was born. It aligns well with growing evidence that the promotion of five fruit and veg per day hasn't really been cutting it. Studies still suggest that five portions of fruit and veg a day can have a positive impact on health but even if you manage it, without the mention of variety, there's an increasing likelihood of often repeating the *same* five fruit and veg. All in, it doesn't deliver anything like the same benefits in areas such as reducing the risk of bowel cancer or improving brain function as the 30-plants-a-week approach.

There is, fairly obviously, much greater nutrient variety in the 30,000 highly diverse species of edible plants available to us than in meat and fish, so it's not a huge surprise that diets rich in different plants are very clearly linked to better health and increased longevity. The Mediterranean Diet, and diets characterised in the Blue Zones (areas where the highest concentration of healthy centenarians live), differ in ingredients, but all follow a predominantly plant-based approach. The gut microbiome of populations like the Hadza in Tanzania have nearly twice the gut microbe diversity that we have in the West, with diets rich in dozens of plants we never eat, and completely lacking in ultra processed foods. The Hadza's risk of common Western disease is greatly reduced.

There are clearly other factors that impact us, but nurturing our gut microbiome makes us more likely to sleep better, move more, benefit from improved mood and energy levels and generally enjoy life more.

It's worth noting, particularly in the context of Hugh's delicious recipes, that spices and herbs all count towards your 30 plants per week. Although they are traditionally used in much smaller quantities than, say, roots or leafy greens, these intensely flavourful aromatic ingredients have a very high concentration of plant chemicals, and so will provide additional benefits when added to our food. A study known as 'the Singapore trial' in 2021 was one of the first to show just how powerful a couple of teaspoonfuls of mixed curry spices per day can be for the gut microbiome. The men in the trial had their microbiome sequenced throughout the trial, and the positive changes in their gut microbe population were impressive, impactful and achieved in only two weeks.

The beauty of changing the message from 'daily fruit and veg' to '30 plants' is that it encourages us to include a much wider variety of foods. Traditional fruits and vegetables are still very much on the menu, but now they have lots of tasty and interesting friends to join them. It's fair to say that many of us hardly ever eat beans and other pulses, whole grains or mushrooms. With 30 plants a week in our sights, we are prompted to be more imaginative and that should have us welcoming some of these wonderful ingredients back onto our plates. It's great to see nuts, seeds and pulses featuring so richly in Hugh's recipes in this book. And you'll also get a boost from knowing that a cup of coffee or tea (especially green tea), a square of dark chocolate and even an occasional glass of wine or cider, will make a positive contribution to your biome.

Eating a wider variety of plants is really about increasing what we offer our gut microbes by adding to what we already eat. This is definitely not about eliminating your firm favourites; if you love celery, apples, bananas, carrots and cucumbers that's wonderful, just don't forget they won't provide everything your gut microbiome needs to be at your optimal health.

A complete and rapid overhaul with lots of unfamiliar plants could be stressful for your gut short term, which is why making simple, easy additions is a good tactic. Including a *sofrito* base in your cooking, with chopped celery, garlic, onions, carrots and sometimes tomatoes, sweated in oil, is a great way to introduce more flavour and fibre, and studies have shown that heated combinations like this release even more healthy polyphenol chemicals for your microbes.

Nuts and seeds are another important high polyphenol addition and have been shown to improve heart disease risk. And alongside ground spice blends, whole seed spices like coriander, cumin, fennel and caraway are all useful as well as being delicious.

For those who really want to maximise the power of vegetables, fermenting them is simple, delicious and adds the benefits of live microbes. Live sauerkrauts and kimchis are widely available in the shops now, but they can also be easily made at home (using the lovely recipes in this book for example). Live fermented vegetables have made a big difference in my life and the science is shaping up to show they are a powerful and effective tool in helping us diversify our gut biome. If you can, I'd recommend eating or drinking something 'live' every day – whether it's a spoonful or two of sauerkraut with your supper, some yoghurt or kefir for breakfast, or a glass of kombucha any time. Or all of the above!

In the past couple of years, I've worked with my team at ZOE, alongside journalists and writers, to show just how straightforward this new 30 plant recommendation can be. What I love about Hugh's cooking is that he makes it easy, enjoyable and delicious to include more plants. I am so pleased that he has brought his flair and unique talent with food to this topic.

Focusing on seasonal fruits and vegetables that naturally add variety through change is a great first step for our planet and our gut microbes. Always having frozen staples to hand, like peas, edamame and sweetcorn, and swapping out different varieties of beans, lentils and other pulses, as well as ringing the changes with nuts, seeds and spices, is an affordable and easy way to integrate more variety.

Simple strategies, which Hugh outlines in this book, like doubling up on alliums and brassicas, or having seed sprinkles like dukka, or mixed nut butters, to hand, make including 30 plants a week in your diet a pleasure and a breeze. Your microbes will love you for it, and the chances are you will rapidly feel the benefits too.

Prof Tim Spector OBE, King's College London, co-founder of ZOE, the personalised nutrition company, and best-selling author of *Food for Life*.

How to Eat More Plants

The brilliant Tim Spector has made a compelling case for the wisdom and benefits of eating 30 plants a week, and now it falls to me to show you how to do it.

Happily, it's a task I relish: not only do I believe I can make it pretty easy for you, I'm also very confident you are going to enjoy the ride. This is partly because I think there is genuine interest, excitement and fun to be had from making this change in your approach to shopping, cooking and eating. But it's mainly because I know that you will end up enjoying your food even more than you already do. Thirty plants a week cannot help but deliver more deliciousness to your plate.

Don't assume that just because this approach is undeniably good for you, it must be a chore to get there. I genuinely think the opposite is true. It frees you from the tyranny of portion size – you can sprinkle on a handful of chopped herbs or a spoonful of sesame seeds and you've chalked up another plant. That's not to say that portion size is never a factor. You know what the good stuff is, and I'd certainly encourage you to eat generous quantities of fresh vegetables: a good handful of wilted, garlicky kale will deliver more goodness than a mere nibble (though even a nibble is better than nothing). On the whole, my recipes here have done the hard work for you, putting glorious fresh veg, fruit, nuts and spices on to your plate in common sense proportions, and with variety and diversity always at their heart.

It is in the world of edible plants that I believe the greatest range of deliciousness is to be found. I say this as an omnivore who still enjoys regular (but by no means daily) helpings of carefully chosen meat and fish. These are special foods, and they appear very temptingly in some of the recipes that follow. In moderation they are good for us. But in terms of sheer variety of flavours, and indeed variety of goodness, they don't come close to what plants can offer. The difference between pork and beef is notable of course, and the difference between lamb and mackerel even more so. But it's nothing compared to the difference between a leek and a walnut, a parsnip and a chilli, or an apple and a coriander seed…

The combining and layering of plants of all kinds has always been at the heart of great cooking, of exciting, delighting and surprising our taste buds (which is one of the defining aspects of human culture, along with art and music). And you are about to spend some time becoming more committed to this central tenet of the culinary art. Enjoy the journey – it's a lifelong pursuit which, like all the best adventures, has no final destination.

A note here also on the parallel joy of thriftiness, and how it can enhance the 30-plants-a-week journey. I've found that including the half red pepper that's sitting in the fridge, a squeeze of juice from yesterday's zested lemon or the handful of cashews at the bottom of the jar adds a new dimension to a dish while also minimising food waste. A leftover plant is still a plant!

You'll also find a list of 'swaps and additions' at the end of many of the recipes in this book – and you should feel free to make any further tweaks that feel right to you!

Most of this book is taken up with 100 recipes that have been created especially to boost the sheer number of plants you are eating. Choose just a few of them each week and you will cross the 30-plants-a-week line easily. And in the next few pages I want to share with you some useful strategies that will help you get there. When I explain them to you as principles that you can apply rather than recipes then you are going to be even better equipped to reach your 30 a week. Adding more plants into your cooking will become second nature. And noting to yourself that you are doing so will be a pleasure in itself.

While the stack of recipes I have coming up for you is going to be a great resource for packing in the plants, 30 plants a week is first and foremost a mindset. Essentially, it's a way of thinking about what you eat. What follows are some useful tips and techniques that will help to set your mind to the task in hand.

Let's get started with a simple exercise:

1 Consider: there are already a lot of plants you like to eat.

2 Admit it, there are a lot of plants you like to eat that you haven't actually eaten for ages!

3 If you're being honest, there are lots of types of plant you hardly ever think of buying at all – the obvious examples for most people being pulses, nuts and seeds, herbs and spices.

4 This is all going to change right now!

One vital thing to draw down from the points above is that the solutions to the 30-plants-a-week challenge are already well within your grasp. I'm not asking you to go in search of a bunch of obscure ingredients or radically change the way you eat. I'm just suggesting you open your eyes a little wider when you shop, cook and eat – scanning for delicious plants at every opportunity.

As Tim mentioned, there are around 11,000 known edible plants. Don't worry, I'm not going to list them all. But I am going to record a very useful bunch of them, in My Big Plant List overleaf. I've divided them into a series of what I consider pragmatic, rather than strictly scientific, categories. There are over 200 in all, so plenty to choose from to comfortably get 30 in every week, whatever the season.

That may sound like a lot – but I'd be surprised if there's anything here you've never heard of. And surprised if there are more than a few plants you've never tasted. But I bet there are loads on this list that have fallen off your radar. For now, just pick a few to put on your next shopping list.

Almost all of the plants listed, by the way, feature in at least one recipe in this book (though some may feature as swaps or optional ingredients). The main exceptions are the tropical fruits. I don't go big on them in my recipes, being such a fan of the gorgeous seasonal fruits and berries we grow in the UK. But I certainly won't begrudge you a ripe mango or a tangy kiwi, and they definitely count as plants!

A pleasing outcome of this exercise is that my list has broken down into 30 categories of plants. I'm not going to suggest you eat one from each category every week… that would be a little obsessive and not wholly practical. But it feels serendipitous and hopefully encouraging to see the usefulness and validity of our favourite new number, albeit from a slightly different angle.

I reckon it's a good idea to revisit My Big Plant List regularly and remind yourself what you've been missing out on. Then you can decide to put a few of them on your shopping list for the following week.

The other thing I hope this list will help you to realise, is that it's actually no great stretch to use and enjoy quite a lot more than 30 plants a week. And that would be very good news indeed.

My Big Plant List

1 Leafy Greens
Cabbages (including
   Spring Greens)
Kales
Spinach
Chard
Pak Choi
Brussels Sprouts
Watercress
Nettles

2 Brassica Sprouts
Calabrese Broccoli
Purple Sprouting Broccoli
Cauliflower
Tenderstem Broccoli
Romanesco

3 Roots
Carrots
Beetroot
Parsnips
Celeriac
Swede
Turnips
Jerusalem Artichokes
Kohlrabi
Radishes
Potatoes (*peel on!*)

4 Alliums
Onions
Red Onions
Spring Onions
Garlic
Leeks
Chives
Wild Garlic

**5 Crunchy Stems and
   Leaves**
Celery
Fennel
Asparagus
Chicory
Radicchio
Globe Artichokes

6 Soft Salad Leaves
Lettuces
Baby Spinach
Rocket
Oriental Greens
Pea Shoots
Sorrel

7 Green Beans and Peas
   (*summer only*)
Green (French) Beans
Runner Beans
Mangetout
Broad Beans

8 Handy Frozen Veg
Peas
Sweetcorn
Spinach
Edamame Beans
Broad Beans

**9 Cucurbits and
   Aubergines**
Cucumber
Courgettes
Pumpkin and Squash
Aubergines

10 Tomatoes
Fresh
Tinned
Passata
Sun-dried

11 Avocados
Avocado!

12 Peppers and Chillies
Green, Red and Yellow Peppers
Romano (long) Peppers
Chillies (red and green)

13 Mushrooms
Flat
Button
Chestnut
Portobello
Oyster
Shiitake
King Oyster
Wild Mushrooms
Dried Porcini

14 Preserved Veg
   (*in vinegar or oil*)
Olives
Capers
Gherkins
Pickled Onions
Pickled Beetroot
Artichoke Hearts

15 Leafy, Salady Herbs
Parsley
Mint
Chives
Coriander
Basil
Rocket
Nasturtiums (leaves/flowers)
Dill
Tarragon

16 Pungent Herbs
Rosemary
Thyme
Bay Leaves
Oregano/Marjoram
Sage

17 Seaweeds and Shore Veg
Nori Sheets
Sea Lettuce
Dulse
Kelp
Seaweed
Samphire

18 Everyday Fruit Bowl
Apples
Pears
Plums
Bananas/Plantains
Grapes
Cherries

19 Citrus Fruits
Lemons
Oranges
Clementines, Easy Peelers etc
Limes
Grapefruit

20 Summer Berries
Strawberries
Raspberries
Blueberries
Blackberries
Blackcurrants/Redcurrants/
   White Currants
Gooseberries

Rhubarb (*honorary fruit!*)

21 Mediterranean/ Exotic Fruit Bowl
Peaches
Nectarines
Melon
Watermelon
Apricots
Figs
Kiwi Fruit
Mango
Pomegranate
Papaya
Passion Fruit
Pineapple

22 Dried Fruits
Raisins
Sultanas
Dried Apricots
Prunes
Dried Apple
Dried Pear
Dates
Dried Figs
Cranberries

23 Nuts
Peanuts
Hazelnuts
Walnuts
Almonds
Pecans
Brazil Nuts
Pine Nuts
Cashews
Chestnuts
Pistachios

24 Tinned Pulses
Butter Beans
Chickpeas
Cannellini Beans
Flageolet Beans
Black Beans
Red Kidney Beans
Borlotti Beans
Pinto Beans
Carlin Peas
Black-eyed Beans
Mung Beans
Aduki Beans
   (and any other beans!)

25 Dried Pulses
Red Lentils
Puy Lentils
Green Lentils
Brown Lentils
Yellow Split Peas

26 Whole Grains (plus Grain Flours, Bread and Pasta)
Wheat
Oats
Barley
Spelt
Rye
Brown Rice
Quinoa
Cornmeal (Polenta)
Buckwheat
Bulgar Wheat

27 Seeds
Sunflower
Pumpkin
Sesame (and Tahini)
Poppy
Flax
Chia
Hemp

28 Spices

Black Pepper
Cumin
Coriander
Caraway
Chilli Flakes (with seeds)
Paprika
Fennel Seeds
Nutmeg
Allspice
Cardamom
Cinnamon
Turmeric (including fresh)
Ginger (including fresh)
Mustard (seeds, and jars of
 ready-made)

**29 Unrefined Oils
(extra virgin/
cold-pressed)**

Olive
Rapeseed
Coconut
Sunflower
Sesame (toasted)
Walnut
Hemp

30 Stimulants

Coffee
Black Tea
Green Tea
Dark/Raw Chocolate
Cacao/Cocoa/Chocolate

So, there you have it: a couple of hundred plants or so… The number is not precise because there are a few repeats across the categories. And there is always the question of how much you want to distinguish between different types of very similar plants.

You'll notice that my mushroom listing is pretty detailed, and I differentiate between fresh, tinned and sun-dried tomatoes, but I don't go so far as to spell out the 12 different varieties of fresh tomato I grew in my greenhouse this summer, or the 4 or 5 different types of kale you can now buy in UK supermarkets, let alone the dozens of different apple varieties you might find if you take the trouble to seek them out.

All of the different varieties of individual plants definitely do offer subtly different spectrums of nutrients, so mixing them up is never a bad idea. But, for the sake of simplicity, we're just going to count apples as apples, and kale as kale, when we tot up our 30.

The take-home here is that there are loads of accessible, affordable plants, fresh and dried, frozen and tinned, pickled and even fermented, sitting on the shelves of a shop not far from you. Right now, you are probably only taking home a fraction of that rich bounty – but this can and will change!

How you're going to make that happen depends to some extent on your personality type, and how you like to get stuff done. Are you an impulsive doer, or a premeditating list maker? Do you like to style it out, or write it down?

Whatever your answer, let's not make this too complicated. One way or another, you're heading to the shops (or your favourite grocery website) with some new items on your shopping list, or with much wider eyes roaming over the goods displayed in front of you, or with a healthy mix of both those things.

To inform your next plant-boosted shopping list, and raise your excitement levels about what's on it, I think it's helpful to share some ideas that should get you well along the road.

And if you want then to go one step further and count every last one of those 30 (plus) plants into your shopping trolley, back to your cupboard and fridge, thence to your pots, pans and roasting trays, and finally down your grateful gullet, I'll happily support that approach. That's why the last of my 10 steps suggests a few simple ways you can keep an accurate weekly tally of your journey to 30 plants, and beyond.

At which point, I think you'll find the first 9 steps have got you there anyway…

Ten Steps to 30 Plants a Week

1 Spend some time with this book

I would say that, wouldn't I? But now you have this book in your hands, I want you to put it to work. Please browse and ruminate. Check out a few recipes and make a (mental or actual) note of the ones that take your fancy.

Then go back to my Big Plant List (pages 14–16) and take stock. If you want to put a ring around the plants that call to you, please do. Likewise, feel free to underline, put scribbles in the margin, or fold down the corners of the recipe pages that take your fancy.

2 No need to be exhaustive

There is a slight caveat to the above. By all means 'stock up', but if you are choosing some plant ingredients that you haven't worked with much, or for a while, don't get too carried away.

Better to choose two or three types (each) of beans/nuts/seeds/spices that you like the look of and are fairly confident in using (perhaps having noted a few recipes in the chapters that follow that call for their use).

The ideal is to build up, over a few weeks, a fairly fast-moving rolling roster of really useful store-cupboard ingredients, that you crack through easily and enthusiastically.

When it comes to fresh vegetables in particular, it's great to set your sights on upping both the variety and the quantity you are eating. But overstocking on produce that you won't get round to eating while it's still really fresh is a quick route to wasting food, and that will be demoralising, potentially undermining your sense that you've really got this 30-plant-a-week thing in hand. Having said that, recipes like my Super six standby supper soup (page 67) and Double and squeak (page 89) are great receivers of leftovers, both raw and cooked.

3 Eat more nuts and seeds

This is right up there because it's an easy win in an area where many of us, even if we really like eating nuts and seeds, somehow often fall short.

We can all be bolder in the way we use nuts and seeds in our cooking. Although they have a shelf life, it's usually measured in months, rather than days, making them forgiving ingredients to keep to hand. They are such fantastically nutritious things, with a potent combination of healthy fats, fibre and protein.

Nuts and seeds are also stunningly versatile, crossing over from sweet to savoury effortlessly, and proving their worth in a huge bandwidth of culinary roles, whether they're being sprinkled over salads, stirred into curries or baked into puds and treats.

Sprinkles and combinations of different nuts and seeds are a particularly easy win. My Nutty seedy clusters (page 204), Toasted tamari seed sprinkle (page 209) and all-purpose Dukka (page 209) are all brilliantly versatile and super useful, and they pop up as optional extras in many recipes. And my Nut and seed butter (page 213) can inveigle its way into all sorts of toothsome corners as an ingredient, as well as being delicious simply spread on toast!

4 Use your freezer

Frozen vegetables are a terrific asset for the 30-plant-a-week cook because they are always to hand, and you can take what you need with minimal waste (I use rubber bands, or those plastic 'clip-it' things, to reseal opened bags of frozen veg).

The mindset shift is to start thinking of frozen veg not so much as easy bits on-the-side for conventional meat-and-two-veg plates of food, but a versatile bunch of ingredients that can find their way into many different multi-plant dishes, especially soups, stews, risottos and the like. I'm quite often near the end of a dish when I find myself thinking, 'I could throw a handful of frozen peas into that', and I quite often do!

There are dozens of frozen veg available, and I would encourage you to experiment widely with them. That said, in my experience some are more useful, versatile and delicious than others. These are the ones that bounce back from freezing to a quality of texture and flavour not so far removed from their character when cooked from fresh. You'll see from the list on page 14 that my five personal favourites are: peas, edamame beans, sweetcorn, broad beans and spinach.

5 Double (and treble) your alliums

If you are sweating some onions for a dish, and not adding some garlic alongside, then I would argue that you are missing an opportunity. If you also happen to have a leek handy, why not chop it up and add it too?

This family of pungent plants has become central to providing a backbone of flavour to dishes from all over the world. They are also full of good things, including fibre, vitamins and anti-inflammatory phytochemicals which help to promote healthy cell development.

Yesterday I made a soup – a variation of the Super six standby supper soup on page 67 that included shallots, onions, garlic and leeks, just because I happened to have all four in the kitchen. And I couldn't resist snipping some chives from the garden in at the end! It was possibly my first ever quintet of alliums, but certainly not my last.

Here's a tip from nutritionist Dr Federica Amati, who has been kind enough to read this text: 'When you are preparing alliums for cooking, if you leave them after chopping, and before cooking, for 10 minutes or so, it helps to fix and preserve sulphur compound phytochemicals and other key nutrients.'

6 Go big on brassicas

The mantra to 'eat your greens' is certainly backed up by nutritional science. These are among the most nutrient dense of all the plants we can eat. They have plenty of fibre and contain a range of phytochemicals called glucosinolates, known for their anti-inflammatory properties. Most brassicas are rich in vitamin K, which is important for blood clotting and bone health, as well as folate, which is a B vitamin critical for building red blood cells and supporting the nervous system. They are also a great source of vitamin C.

Brassicas are also, mostly, inexpensive and accessible. Across the dozens of different varieties of cabbages, kales, caulis, broccolis and sprouts that we grow in the UK, brassicas in some form are available throughout the year. (It's worth noting that rocket, watercress and pak choi are all members of this family too.)

That doesn't make brassicas everyone's favourite veg. But it does mean it's well worth exploring different ways to enjoy them, and settling on a few that really float your boat. Stirring greens through a lemony polenta (as pictured opposite) is one of my all-time favourites (see page 199).

When I was growing up Mum served us greens, lightly buttered on the side of my plate. She was never one to overcook them, but recognised that steaming or wilting the greens just long enough to make them tender is the best way to retain their appealing sweetness – and their goodness too, by the way. She still does, and so do I from time to time. A tip to maximise the appeal of this approach is to gently sizzle a grated clove of garlic in a little butter or oil and toss with the tender greens. This works for green beans, peas and even carrots, and can be effective in tempting kids to eat more veg.

Having said that, these days I'm more likely to use the greens as an 'ingredient', mingled with other delicious things. There are a lot of recipes in this book that do this, and you'll find plenty of brassicas and greens in my soups, suppers, stews and sides, and in a good many of my roasting trays too. Head straight for the Roast brassicas and butter beans (page 165) if you want to reel in a trio of brassicas in one gorgeously savoury roasting tray.

Another great way to enjoy brassicas is as part of a delicious live fermented sauerkraut or kimchi. Fermenting raw vegetables preserves their nutrients better than cooking them and, in some cases – with vitamin C for example – makes them even more 'bio-available'. I've been making my own krauts and live ferments for a few years now, and find it a fun process, with very delicious results. If you fancy giving it a go, try the recipes on pages 227–30.

7 Have a bean feast

Most of us could happily get more beans, lentils and chickpeas into our cooking. They are so good for us, containing plenty of plant protein, fibre and micro-nutrients like iron and some B vitamins. And they're particularly helpful when we are looking to reduce the amount of meat we eat (a good idea for so many reasons). They are also great for filling us up.

If you like eating pulses, but just don't get round to it very often, this is an easy fix. In fact, you've just decided to fix it, right? But if you are something of a pulse sceptic (perhaps because you think beans and lentils are a bit

boring and bland) how can I persuade you to think differently? Perhaps you could stop thinking about them in isolation, as boring beans in a tin, or a virtue-signalling pile of lentils on the side of a plate? Start mingling them in your mind with other delicious ingredients, just as I've mingled them in all sorts of saucy ways in the recipes that follow.

Check out the following colourful and flavour-packed recipes: Squash mulligatawny (page 58), Herby bean and celery salad (page 92), Nutty seedy hummus (page 214), Aubergine cassoulata (page 169) and Slow-roast Merguez-spiced shoulder of lamb (page 140). Not to mention Root and rosemary hot pot (page 170), pictured opposite, which features butter beans, one of my favourite pulses, along with a medley of roots.

Recipes with pulses are great, but once you get into the swing of it, improvising with them is also a blast, because they are so fantastically easy to use. Just open a tin! Tinned pulses are minimally processed and retain all the goodness you would get by cooking them.

To be properly tender and palatable, dried beans need to be soaked overnight and boiled for an hour and more. I still do that sometimes, but much more often I use beans from tins.

Lentils, on the other hand, I generally cook from scratch. Most lentil varieties can be cooked to tender in 20 minutes or less (soaking them for an hour is a useful preliminary). But tinned lentils are also very handy.

8 Snack the difference

There is no shame whatsoever in allowing a little healthy snacking to help get you over the 30 plants line in any given week. And there's no doubt in my mind which are the best food groups that are going to help you do this: nuts and seeds, of course; raw veg; seasonal fresh and dried fruits (the latter in moderation, as they have quite high concentrated sugars). And why not just a little dark chocolate?

To keep your snacking healthy and plant-based, and to avoid the temptation to grab something manufactured when you're on the go, it helps to prep ahead. When I'm travelling for work, I often take with me a little tin of my seven-plant Trail mix (page 206). And if I've got a few minutes in the morning, I'll also do a tub of Crunchy veg to go (page 206). Carrots, celery, fennel and a few wedges of apple is a favourite combo. You can tip a few nuts and seeds in too, or even a sprinkling of herbs or whole seed spices.

9 Have herbs handy

Both fresh and dried herbs are delightful for adding depth and flavour to all kinds of dishes. As Tim points out on page 8, even in the relatively small quantities that we tend to use them, they really do count, as they are often packed with micro-nutrients that are scarce in other plants.

I think many of us tend to use herbs only when we are cooking a recipe in which they are specified. I'd encourage you to use them more freely than that. Tossing some parsley leaves into any salad, scattering some fresh coriander onto a spicy soup, or snipping some chives onto your scrambled eggs will only enhance the result.

Of course, the best way to have fresh herbs handy is to grow them. Even if you don't have space for a veg patch, a few pots or containers, or even a window box, can yield a meaningful harvest, as well as giving great satisfaction. If your space, and time, is limited, I'd recommend growing a small number of herbs in reasonable quantities, rather than trying to grow smaller amounts of lots of different herbs.

A good-sized (ideally at least 10-litre) pot of well-established mint, parsley or chives should yield a generous couple of picks per week in the summer. The more pungent 'hard herbs', such as rosemary and thyme, are effective in smaller quantities anyway, and are relatively low-maintenance, once established. And it's

exactly these five herbs that I would prescribe as most useful and easiest to grow. You'll see them cropping up a lot in my recipes ahead.

10 By all means, keep your score!

We've come all this way, exploring some strategies and attitudes that I'm confident will help you arrive at, if not sail past, the 30-plants-a-week objective. So, let's end with a note on the most infallible way to ensure you really are making progress. Count the plants you eat!

With that in mind, you might have spotted that My Big Plant List not only appears in the middle of this opening chapter, it's reproduced as the 'endpaper' at the front and back of this book. For these versions, I've even put 5 handy boxes next to each plant, to help you keep a record of the plants you are eating for the first 5 weeks of your 30-plant journey. Thereafter, I'm confident you'll be clocking up your 30, and more, with minimal effort, and maximum pleasure. But you can always come back to this list, perhaps monthly, rather than weekly, and check your score.

Oh, and just in case you were wondering, you can only count each plant once in a week – by all means count it again the following week! So, if you are currently eating carrots or kale, or walnuts or even watercress twice, or indeed several times a week, then that's *great*. But you only get to count it once.

So please, set to with a pencil and see how much fun counting your plant intake can actually be. You may very well be impressed at how many plants you are already consuming, and I'm sure this will inspire you to take in even more! It's always rewarding to mark your progress, see your list of plants eaten grow longer every week, and note to yourself how much you are enjoying them too.

You don't have to use this book for your plant list, you can also use your phone or a laptop, or just freestyle it in a notebook. If you take this approach, it's handy to start with a list of the plants you are confident you are eating pretty much every week. (Are there a couple you can add to these stalwarts, forever? In my case, not a week goes by without me munching a few pumpkin seeds, and a tin of butter beans. That certainly wasn't the case a few years ago.) With these dependables banked, you only need to write down the weekly extras…

However you choose to keep the score, if you get past 20 plants in a week (you absolutely will!) you'll immediately have 30 in your sights. I'm sure you're already thinking about recipes you know you love to cook. What extra plant ingredients could you add to these? If you're a keen baker, what seeds or nuts could you throw into your bread, or even cakes? If you like spices, what useful ones are missing from your spice rack? When did you last cook parsnips or cauliflower, which actually you love!

You're already thinking like a 30-plants-a-week eater, and I'm betting that next week, you simply won't be able to stop yourself from overhauling that magic number… So that's how you can make this happen. Now it's over to you.

I know you are going to enjoy broadening your diet by upping your plants, week by week. The recipes that follow are here to make that even easier. You will see that most of the recipe chapter headings include a number – Magnificent Seven Salads, for example – which is the minimum number of plants contained in every recipe within that chapter, and most of them contain several more.

I can pretty much guarantee that if you cook just three or four of my recipes in any given week, you'll soon be shooting past the 30 plants target. But just to make *sure* you do, I've gathered some 3-recipe combos overleaf that will *definitely* get you past the magic number. All you have to do is cook (and eat!) each of the dishes at some point during the week.

10 x 3 recipes per week to GUARANTEE your 30 plants

31 plants

Hard-boiled breakfast
(page 44)

Very veggie double dhal
(page 86)

Slow-roast Merguez-spiced
shoulder of lamb
(page 140)

34 plants

Purple shakshuka
(page 42)

Creamy roast cauli and
cashew soup (page 57)

Roast chicken and veg
with herby brown rice
(page 134)

33 plants

Green eggs with halloumi
and herbs (page 41)

Roast brassicas and butter beans
(page 165)

Sausage and lentils with
apple and sage
(page 139)

35 plants

Festive cabbage and
clementine salad (page 108)

Festive spiced stuffed squash
(page 176)

Nutty seedy clusters
(page 204)

30 plants

Celeriac, crispy quinoa and
goat's cheese (page 173)

Barley kedgerotto (page 127)

Cottage garden pie
(page 152)

38 plants

Roast ratatouille mackerel fillets (page 124)

Big green summer salad (page 100)

Nutty seedy hummus (page 214)

30 plants

Beans, greens, pasta and pesto (page 82)

Spicy fish fillet parcels (page 128)

Courgette meatballs in barley broth (page 145)

33 plants

Gazpacho (page 62)

Creamy, lemony, minty courgettes (page 192)

Charred veg with seaweed gribiche (page 70)

33 plants

Baked fresh and dried fruit compote (page 34)

Black bean, corn and tomato soup (page 65)

Rooty fish cakes with seeded crumb crust (page 122)

31 plants

Rustic on-the-bone chicken korma (page 136)

Aubergine cassoulata (page 169)

Tutti-frutti semifreddo (page 243)

Five for Breakfast and Brunch

What we choose to eat at the start of the day is heavily influenced by tradition, and most of the time we don't question where that tradition comes from, or how much wisdom it embodies. Many of us are still eating and drinking what our parents gave us for breakfast, and what TV advertising, sitcoms and soaps have insinuated it means: cereals, toast and orange juice.

Of course, there is a lot of comfort in tradition, and in the familiarity that comes with repetition. There's also some decent nutrition in the best kind of cereals (i.e. wholegrain-based with minimal processing or additives). They offer us complex carbs that give us slow-release energy through the morning, soluble fibre to feed our gut microbiome (not to mention reducing bad LDL cholesterol), and often seeds and dried fruit too.

But if you've already cast your eye over my list of 30 plant-based food groups, you might find it striking that, when it comes to breakfast, most of us draw on so few of them. This may be because breakfast time, during the week anyway, can be rushed, busy and slightly chaotic. But if you eat the same thing for breakfast, day in day out, you're missing out on a great opportunity to diversify your diet. Even shaking up the routine once or twice during the week can really boost your plant count.

I have always enjoyed fruit for breakfast, and from early autumn to early spring often one of the first things I eat is an apple. A whole piece of fruit is a much better breakfast choice than fruit juice, which contains 'free' sugars. These may be natural but they are no longer bound up with the fibre of the whole fruit, so tend to make blood sugar rise fairly quickly.

Add some nuts and seeds to your fruity day-starter and the healthy fats and extra fibre will complement your digestion and reduce the risk of a blood-sugar spike followed by an energy crash. That's why this chapter begins with simple ideas for fruit and nut plates. They're barely recipes – I just want to put ideas in your head!

Recent research suggests that bitter and sour food and drinks can aid the digestive process by stimulating saliva production – things like tea and coffee, grapefruit and other citrus, but also tart drinks like kombucha or a ginger-based tea, bitter-sweet nuts such as walnuts, and even leaves like radicchio and rocket. Beginning your day with a few sharper flavours literally gets your juices flowing and that can, over time, have a very positive impact on digestion because it keeps everything moving. The saliva we produce when we munch on whole fruits also kick-starts the digestive process – another reason to forgo fruit juice for the real-deal whole fruit!

I urge porridge fans to give my multigrain version (on page 31) a go. Simply putting more grains in the mix, plus some nuts and seeds, can help us to digest carbohydrates more slowly, and maximise the nutritional uptake of these foods. And I suggest you deploy the same tactic with my overnight oats (on page 32), incorporating tasty, flaked grains like barley or quinoa flakes, as well as fruit, seeds and even root veg.

Many people are now choosing to start the day with savoury foods that lean more towards protein than carbs, and I am happy to join their ranks – at least a few days a week. You cannot beat an egg (or two) for complete protein and a healthy dose of essential fatty acids. They're quick to cook and partner so well with all kinds of veg.

For a relatively speedy breakfast, try poached, fried or scrambled eggs on top of a thick layer of leafy pesto, or perhaps a generous spoonful of a kraut or kimchi (see page 227–8), on wholegrain toast. Or boil a couple of eggs the night before and you're ready for my Hard-boiled breakfast (page 44).

There is also the question of *when* you have breakfast. I'm keen on extending the time I eat nothing at all – the overnight fast – at least a couple of times a week, in a very flexible version of intermittent fasting. And the closer breakfast gets to lunch, the more it starts looking like lunch too! Hence there are some brunchy offerings, such as my delicious gram flour pancakes, with the veg-packed fattoush filling (on page 39). Or my potently Purple shakshuka (page 42).

You will find the breakfasts right here are all built on at least five plants. Vegetables like carrots, beetroot, celery and spinach come into play as well as the more traditional fruits and grains. There are tons of nuts and seeds too – adding fibre and flavour and healthy fats, as well as some irresistible crunch.

I really hope you'll find something here to tempt you off the well-trodden breakfast pathways and into the adventurous realms of starting the day with many more plants!

Fruit and Nut Plates

Multigrain Porridge

Lunchbox Overnight Oats

Fruit Compotes

Proteinaceous Pancakes

Green Eggs with Halloumi and Herbs

Purple Shakshuka

Hard-boiled Breakfast

Porridge Loaf

Lemon and Spice Tea with Bircher Finish

Chocolate, Coffee and Turmeric Booster

Fruit and Nut Plates

Once or twice a week I like to start the day with a simple plate of fruit and nuts or nut butter. It's a delicious combination, and the fatty, fibrous nuts slow down the sugar spike we might get from eating fruit on its own. Sometimes I'll munch an apple at my desk while also dipping into a bowl of nuts and raisins. But it's also nice to put together a plate with at least five different items going on… and taking your time to enjoy the combinations.

I like mixing fresh and dried fruits – munching a slice of apple with a walnut half and a few raisins on it, for example, or popping a couple of pumpkin seeds on top of a clementine slice, or sticking a sunflower seed inside a raisin! You can soak the nuts and seeds overnight if you like – it makes them plump and juicy, almost as if they've been freshly picked. There are endless combinations, but here are a couple of my favourites: one vaguely autumn/ winter, the other summery. You'll notice I include cucumber as a fruit – which of course it is!

Apples, Nuts and Seeds

Serves 1

1 crisp eating apple, such as Cox or Braeburn, or a fairly firm pear
1 clementine or easy peeler, or a few grapes
A handful of walnuts or almonds
A handful of raisins or a couple of dried apricots
A scattering of pumpkin or sunflower seeds

Cut the apple into slim wedges, whittling out the pippy bit. Peel the clementine, if using, and slice into rounds, or simply divide into segments. Pile the fresh fruit on a plate and scatter over the nuts, dried fruit and seeds. Eat with your fingers in varying combinations. It really is that simple, but it's also surprisingly delicious and fun!

Swaps
Stick to an apple or a pear and swap around the nuts and dried fruits as much as you like. You can also use the Nutty seedy clusters on page 204 instead of raw nuts and seeds.

Berries with Nut Butter

Serves 1

100g strawberries, halved if large
A handful of blueberries and/or raspberries (optional)
½ small cucumber, cut into sticks
2–3 tsp Nut and seed butter (page 213)

Put the berries and cucumber on a plate with a blob of nut and seed butter. Eat with your fingers and/or a fork, dipping or squashing the fruits into the nut butter.

Swaps
Serve Sunflower and oat cream (page 220) instead of the nut and seed butter. Whole nuts and seeds, especially when pre-soaked overnight in water to plump them up, are another great option to eat with the berries.

Multigrain Porridge

Boost the plant count in your porridge mix with a few extra flaked grains to get the most out of your breakfast. I have a jar on the shelf that has a mix of oats, flakes and flaxseed. You can also add some chia seeds and/or ground hemp or flax seeds too.

6–8 servings

300g porridge oats (not jumbo)
100g barley or spelt flakes
100g quinoa or rye flakes
50g hemp kernels or ground
  flaxseed (optional)
50g chia seeds (optional)

To cook

125ml milk, or nut/oat milk
  (optional)
A pinch of salt (optional)

To finish
Choose from:
A little cold milk
A trickle of honey or maple syrup,
  or a sprinkling of brown sugar
A handful of mixed seeds
  (untoasted) and dried fruit
Nutty seedy clusters (page 204)
Any fruit compote (pages 34
  and 237)

Combine the porridge oats with the other flakes and seeds if using, and store in a large airtight container or jar. This mix will then be ready to go whenever you need it.

When you are ready to cook, weigh out 60g per person of the dry mix (3–4 tbsp if you're feeling relaxed), tip into a pan and add 125ml milk and 125ml water (or use all milk or all water if you prefer). Add a pinch of salt if you like – to enhance the grains' natural flavours.

Place the pan over a medium-low heat and let the porridge come gradually to a simmer, stirring often with a wooden spoon or spurtle; this will take a couple of minutes. Let it gently simmer for another minute or two, stirring often, until thickened.

If the porridge is thicker than you like to eat it, add a dash of water – hot from the kettle if that's handy. If you think it looks a touch on the loose side, don't panic. It will start to thicken up a bit as soon as you put it into a bowl.

Ladle the porridge into a bowl, and the rest is up to you. A dash of cold milk is nice to cool it down a touch. For sweetness (and you would have to be very austere to enjoy your porridge totally unsweetened), I like a trickle of honey, but you might prefer brown sugar or maple syrup.

A scattering of seeds or dried fruit adds goodness and interest, and there are plenty of other goodies that could also be added, for example nutty seedy clusters and/or a spoonful of fruit compote.

Lunchbox Overnight Oats

This semi-savoury take on overnight oats can be breakfast, brunch or lunch, and works particularly well as an 'eat at your desk' power snack. The inclusion of root veg and oil sounds quirky but makes it really delicious, as well as adding extra fibre and goodness.

3–4 servings

1 medium-large carrot
1 medium eating apple or firm
  pear
50g chopped walnuts
50g sunflower and/or pumpkin
  seeds
1 tsp caraway or fennel seeds
100g porridge oats (or use the
  multigrain mix on page 31)
50g raisins, sultanas or dried
  cranberries
3 tbsp extra virgin olive or
  rapeseed oil
Finely grated zest and juice of
  ½ lemon
200ml cloudy apple juice
Sea salt and black pepper
  (optional)

Peel the carrot only if the skin looks a bit tired, otherwise just wash it, then grate coarsely into a large bowl. Grate the apple or pear, skin on, directly into the bowl.

Add all the remaining ingredients, including a pinch of salt and a few grinds of pepper (if you want to emphasise the savoury elements). Mix together well, making sure the grated fruit and veg are well distributed and coated with the liquid.

Cover the bowl and leave in the fridge for at least a couple of hours, ideally overnight. Stir well in the morning, adding an extra dash of apple juice or water if you think it looks a bit dry, and bring it back up to room temperature before eating.

If you're taking your oats to work, pack a generous portion straight from the fridge in a leakproof container, and eat within a few hours.

Swaps
Instead of the carrot, try grated parsnip or celeriac – or beetroot, for a splendidly colourful option. You can also swap the apple or pear with a couple of finely chopped plums. Vary the dried fruit as you like: chopped apricots, dried cherries, sliced dates and prunes are all great. And ring the changes with the nuts: whole or roughly chopped hazelnuts, pecans and almonds are all good alternatives to the walnuts.

Fruit Compotes

Here are two easy ways to make fruit compotes that are delicious with Multigrain porridge (page 31), Nutty seedy clusters (page 204) or yoghurt, or all of these. They are also great spooned onto rice pudding, or topped with crumble (on page 234) for a snack or simple pud.

The first bakes fresh and dried fruits together with a little cider vinegar. The second simply rehydrates dried fruits in kombucha. Both compotes are equally delicious, tangy and great for gut health.

Baked Fresh and Dried Fruit Compote

Serves 4–6 *(with other things)*

1kg plums or apricots, halved and stoned
2 crisp, tart eating apples, such as Cox, Russet or Braeburn, halved, cored and cut into wedges
150g mixed dried fruit, such as apricots (unsulphured), prunes, raisins and sultanas
1 orange
200ml green, black or herbal tea
4 tbsp apple cider vinegar (ideally raw)

Preheat the oven to 200°C/180°C Fan/Gas 6.

Place the plum or apricot halves, cut side up, in a fairly deep ovenproof dish with the apple wedges and dried fruit, to fit snugly in a layer (so the fruit cooks in the juices and doesn't dry out).

Finely grate the zest from the orange over the fruit, then halve the orange and squeeze the juice over the fruit too. Pour on the tea and cider vinegar.

Place the dish in the oven and bake for 25–30 minutes, giving it a stir halfway through, until everything is soft and the dried fruit has soaked up some of the juices.

Serve warm or cold, with porridge and/or nutty seedy clusters, crumble, rice pudding etc, spooning over yoghurt or kefir if you like.

This compote will keep in a jar or container in the fridge for a week.

Kombucha and Dried Fruit Compote

Makes 1 large jar

300g mixed dried fruit, such as apricots (unsulphured), prunes, apples, pears, figs, cranberries, cherries, raisins and sultanas (ideally at least 5 types)
250–300ml kombucha

Put your chosen dried fruit into a very clean large jar or container (500ml capacity) and pour over the live kombucha, making sure it covers all the fruit. Put the lid on then place in the fridge for at least 24 hours.

The compote will keep in the fridge for a couple of weeks and the dried fruit will become more tender as time goes on.

Swaps
Instead of kombucha, use green tea or a herbal tea, brewed then cooled, with 1 tbsp apple cider vinegar added for a bit of tartness.

Proteinaceous Pancakes

These lovely pancakes are made with half gram (chickpea) flour and half fine plain wholemeal flour. They also work well with 'ancient grain' flours like spelt, einkorn and khorasan. They have a little more protein and fibre than a plain white pancake, and a lovely nutty flavour. They are particularly good for brunch with savoury fillings like the fattoush and wilted greens (overleaf). But they're also delicious with fruit fillings, like the apple (below). The batter keeps for 4 days in the fridge, so I often make double and bash out pancakes with different fillings over a few days. Use plant-based milk and omit the egg for a vegan version. I usually make my filling(s) before I cook the pancakes, while the batter is resting. But if you are frying eggs to top off savoury pancakes, then it makes sense to cook the pancakes first.

Makes 5–6

100g gram flour
100g light wholemeal flour (or
  spelt, einkorn or khorasan)
A pinch of salt
1 medium egg (optional)
250–300ml milk (dairy or nut/
  oat milk)
1 tsp sugar or runny honey (for
  a sweet pancake, optional)
Oil or fat for cooking

To make the batter, sift the flours and salt together into a bowl and make a well in the middle. Add the egg, if using, then pour in the milk little by little, whisking until you have a smooth batter, the consistency of single cream. If you're not using an egg, you'll need a little more milk. If you're making a sweet pancake, you can whisk in the sugar or honey. Ideally, let the batter rest for 10–20 minutes.

To cook the pancakes, place a medium frying pan or crêpe pan over a fairly high heat and add a little oil or fat to give a very fine film over the base of the pan. Pour in a small ladleful of batter, swirling the pan as you do, so you get an even thin layer (a shade thicker than a classic crêpe), pouring out any excess batter.

Cook for about 2 minutes, until the underside is golden, then flip the pancake and cook the other side for a minute or two. Tip onto a plate and repeat, stacking the pancakes as you go. You may want to add a touch more oil or fat after the third or fourth pancake.

Apple, Nut and Raisin Filling

Fills 5–6 pancakes

2 medium eating apples, such
  as Cox or Braeburn
A little butter or oil for frying
1 tsp soft light brown sugar
50g raisins
30g walnuts or hazelnuts,
  roughly chopped
Grated zest and juice of ½ lemon
2 tbsp Nut and seed butter
  (page 213, optional)
Natural yoghurt to serve (optional)

Quarter and core the apples, then cut each quarter into 2 or 3 slices. Heat the butter or oil in a frying pan over a medium heat then add the apples and fry gently for a couple of minutes.

Add the sugar and raisins to the pan, along with the nuts. Cook for a further 5–6 minutes until the apples are tender, golden and glazed, and the raisins have plumped nicely. Add the lemon zest and juice and toss to get a little sauce going.

Dot each pancake with nut butter if you like, before spooning on the fruit filling. You can either fold the pancake in half over the filling or leave the pancake open to show off the filling. Serve with yoghurt if you like.

Continued overleaf

Fattoush Filling

Fills 3–4 pancakes

1 small fennel bulb (about 120g),
  trimmed
10–12 radishes, thinly sliced
4 spring onions, trimmed and
  finely sliced
1 Little Gem lettuce, shredded
250g cherry tomatoes, quartered
A handful of parsley or mint (or
  both), roughly chopped
A handful of Toasted tamari seed
  sprinkle or Dukka (page 209),
  to finish (optional)

Dressing
Finely grated zest and juice of
  ½ lemon
2 tsp sumac (optional)
50ml olive oil, plus a little to finish
Sea salt and black pepper

Thinly slice the fennel lengthways and place in a large bowl with the other prepared veg and cherry tomatoes.

For the dressing, combine the ingredients thoroughly, either by whisking them together in a small bowl or shaking in a jar, seasoning with salt and pepper to taste.

Pour the dressing over the veg and toss thoroughly to combine. Add most of the chopped herbs, holding a bit back for a sprinkle, and toss through.

Spoon a generous pile of fattoush over one half of each pancake and add a sprinkling of tamari seed sprinkle or dukka if you have some. Fold the sides of the pancakes inwards slightly, to partially enclose the filling. Trickle a little olive oil over the top and finish with a sprinkle of herbs.

Wilted Greens and an Egg

Fills 2 pancakes generously

100g spinach or any seasonal
  greens, such as cavolo nero,
  chard or kale
1 tbsp oil or fat for cooking
A small handful of parsley, finely
  chopped
A small bunch of chives, finely
  chopped
2 eggs
A nugget of Cheddar or
  Parmesan, grated (optional)
Sea salt and black pepper
A handful of Toasted tamari seed
  sprinkle or Dukka (page 209),
  to finish (optional)

Remove any coarse stalks from the spinach or greens and roughly shred the leaves. Heat most of the oil or fat in a medium-large frying pan over a medium heat. Add the greens with three-quarters of the herbs and cook, stirring occasionally, for a few minutes until wilted and tender.

If using spinach and it gives off some water, just tip this out of the pan. Season with a little salt and pepper. Push the greens to the side of the pan to make room for the eggs.

Add a little more fat or oil to the empty area of the pan, then crack in the eggs and fry to your liking. 'Sunny side up' looks best, or you can flip the egg at the end for 20 seconds or so if you prefer 'over easy' eggs. Give the greens a nudge every now and again, just to make sure they don't burn while you are cooking the eggs.

Divide the greens between two pancakes, sprinkle with the grated cheese if using, and place an egg in the middle of each. Scatter over the remaining herbs and some toasted tamari seeds or dukka if you like. Fold the pancakes to partially enclose the filling.

Green Eggs with Halloumi and Herbs

Forget green eggs and ham (at least until you get to the swaps below!) and enjoy your eggs with halloumi and herbs instead. This is a brilliant all-day meal – equally good for brunch, lunch or supper. You can easily scale the quantities down for one, or double them to serve four and cook in two batches. It ticks the boxes for lots of lovely greens, made irresistible with creamy scrambled eggs.

Serves 2

Oil or fat for cooking
100g halloumi, cut into
   small cubes
A bunch of spring onions,
   trimmed and finely sliced
100g kale or spinach, coarse
   stalks removed, roughly
   shredded
A handful of frozen peas
4 eggs
A knob of butter (optional)
Sea salt and black pepper

To finish

A handful of herbs, such as
   chives, parsley or coriander,
   finely chopped
Dukka (page 209, optional)

Heat a little oil or fat in a medium non-stick frying pan over a fairly high heat. Add the halloumi and sizzle until starting to brown on the underside. Turn and cook until golden on the other side.

Add the spring onions and the shredded kale or spinach to the pan and sweat, stirring occasionally, until wilted. Stir in the frozen peas and cook with the greens, tossing or stirring occasionally, for 3–4 minutes until the veg are tender. Tip the veg and halloumi out onto a plate and set aside. Lower the heat under the pan.

Beat the eggs together lightly in a bowl, seasoning with salt and pepper. Add a little extra oil or knob of butter to the pan and once it is melted and foaming, pour in the beaten egg.

As it starts to set at the edges, use a spatula or wooden spoon to stir the set egg back into the wet egg. Keep stirring now and then until the eggs are scrambled as soft or firm as you like.

Add the veg and halloumi back to the pan to warm through then divide between warmed plates. Sprinkle over the chopped herbs, then the dukka if using. Finish with a grinding of black pepper.

Swaps
In place of the kale or spinach, use another leafy green, such as cavolo nero, spring greens or chard, or broccoli florets, roughly chopped.
You can also revive the green eggs and ham concept by sizzling some bacon in place of the halloumi.

Some more quick ways to 'veg-up' your eggs
The classics of the 'eggs on toast' genre can be almost instantly vegged up with the addition of some gorgeous green pesto (see page 216), or a nice spicy kraut or kimchi (see pages 228–30). Just spread the pesto, or pile the kraut/kimchi, generously on wholemeal toast, and top it with 2 eggs, poached, fried or scrambled to your liking.

Purple Shakshuka

Beetroot adds fibre and richness to a classic shakshuka, as well as turning it a fab purple colour. It makes a great breakfast or brunch, or you can serve it up with wholegrain bread or toast for a hearty supper to feed two.

Serves 2 heartily, or 4 lightly

Oil or fat for cooking
1 large or 2 medium-small red or brown onions, finely sliced
2 garlic cloves, finely grated or chopped
1 small red chilli, or a good pinch of dried chilli flakes (optional)
½ tsp cumin seeds
½ tsp smoked paprika, plus an extra pinch
1 medium beetroot, scrubbed and coarsely grated (about 150g)
1 red pepper, cored, deseeded and sliced (optional)
400g tin peeled plum tomatoes
2 tbsp extra virgin olive oil
400g tin kidney beans
1 small radicchio, roughly shredded
4 eggs
Sea salt and black pepper

To serve
50g herb leaves, such as parsley, chives, coriander, chervil or lovage, roughly chopped
Finely grated zest and juice of ½ lemon
1–2 tsp extra virgin olive oil
Dukka (page 209)

Heat a little oil or fat in a medium frying pan, or a shallow, wide, flameproof casserole over a medium heat. Add the onion(s) and fry for 6–8 minutes until soft but not coloured, then add the garlic, chilli, cumin seeds and smoked paprika. Cook, stirring often, for 2 minutes.

Add the beetroot, red pepper if using, and the tinned tomatoes, crushing them with your hands as they go in (and picking out any stalky ends or bits of skin). Cook for 8–10 minutes until the tomatoes start to break down, helping them to do so with the back of the spoon. Stir in the extra virgin olive oil, and a splash of water if the mixture looks at all dry.

Drain the beans, keeping a little of the liquid, then add them to the pan with the saved liquid. Stir in the radicchio and simmer gently for 4–5 minutes, stirring occasionally, until everything is tender, well combined and saucy.

Using the back of a tablespoon, make 4 hollows in the mixture. Crack an egg into each hollow and season with salt, pepper and a pinch of smoked paprika. Turn the heat to low, put the lid on the pan and cook for 4–6 minutes until the egg whites are set but the yolks are still runny.

Meanwhile, in a small bowl, dress the herbs with the lemon zest and juice, a pinch of salt, and the extra virgin olive oil.

Serve the shakshuka as soon as it is ready, with the dressed herbs, and dukka to sprinkle over.

Swaps
Use cannellini, flageolet or butter beans, chickpeas or tinned Puy, green or brown lentils instead of kidney beans.
You can also replace the radicchio with red chicory, Little Gem lettuce, or a large handful of seasonal greens, such as purple or green kale.
If you haven't got a beetroot, you can use a carrot or two instead.

Hard-boiled Breakfast

Here's another proteinaceous savoury breakfast/brunch/lunch for you, based around the delicious combination of creamy hard-boiled eggs and tangy tomatoes, with some other pleasing plants thrown in. There are fun variations to this dish for you to try, too (see swaps, below).

Serves 1

2 medium eggs (at room
   temperature)
A few cherry tomatoes, quartered
2 spring onions, or ¼ small red
   onion, trimmed and sliced
1 celery stick, thinly sliced
⅓ x 400g tin cannellini or other
   tinned beans, drained and
   rinsed
A small bunch of parsley, leaves
   picked, or rocket leaves
2 tbsp extra virgin olive oil
A squeeze of lemon juice or
   ½ tbsp apple cider vinegar
   (ideally raw)
Sea salt and black pepper
Toasted tamari seed sprinkle
   (page 209), to finish (optional)

Bring a small saucepan of water to the boil. Lower the eggs into the pan and boil for 7 minutes for just-gooey yolks in the middle, or up to 10 minutes for firm yolks. Drain and run under cold water until cool enough to handle, then peel the eggs. Leave to cool for a few more minutes (or dip the peeled eggs in cold water if you're in a hurry).

In a bowl, toss the cherry tomatoes, onion(s), celery, tinned beans, parsley or rocket, extra virgin olive oil and lemon juice or cider vinegar together. Season with salt and pepper to taste. Spoon onto a plate.

Halve the boiled eggs, or cut into wedges, and place on top of the salady mix. Add a sprinkle of toasted tamari seeds if you like and serve, ideally without toast.

Swaps and Additions
Replace the celery stick with ½ fennel bulb, trimmed and sliced very thinly.
Add some diced cooked beetroot and a good spoonful of Purple-powered kim-kraut (page 228) instead of (or as well as) the tomatoes.
Scatter a few anchovies over the eggs and salady mix to finish, if you like.
Add ½ small tin of sardines or mackerel fillets in oil to any of the above combinations, plus some capers and chopped gherkins.
Alternatively, add a little chopped leftover meat or sausage.

Five for Breakfast and Brunch

Porridge Loaf

This is a one-bowl, no-knead, gluten-free, fruity, nutty bread (provided you use gluten-free oats) that is unbelievably easy to make. You can use any mix of dried fruit, nuts and seeds that you happen to have in the kitchen – sultanas, raisins, dried apples, dried apricots, dried figs etc – or just nuts and seeds if you want a more savoury loaf.

The loaf is delicious freshly baked, of course, but also excellent toasted the following day. It freezes well too; I often double the quantities to make 2 loaves, one for now and one for the freezer.

I've put it in the breakfast chapter, but as you can imagine it's lovely for tea too – or any other time, frankly. I love it with just a lick of butter, but it's also great with a trickle of honey and rather good with cheese, too.

Makes 1 loaf

250g natural yoghurt
1 medium egg
150g porridge oats
100g mixed dried fruit, larger
 fruits roughly chopped
100g mixed seeds, such as
 pumpkin, sunflower, poppy,
 linseed, or buckwheat, plus an
 extra small handful to finish
50g nuts, such as walnuts,
 hazelnuts, almonds or cashews,
 roughly chopped
1 tsp caraway seeds (optional)
50ml milk
½ tsp bicarbonate of soda
½ tsp flaky sea salt

Preheat the oven to 190°C/170°C Fan/Gas 5. Line a small (500g/1lb) loaf tin with baking paper.

In a large bowl, whisk the yoghurt and egg together until smoothly combined. Stir in all the remaining ingredients until evenly mixed, to give a creamy mixture, the texture of a thick porridge.

Spoon the mixture into the prepared loaf tin and level the surface using the back of the spoon. Scatter a handful of extra seeds evenly over the top.

Place on the middle shelf of the oven and bake for 45–50 minutes until a deep golden brown.

Allow the loaf to cool in the tin for 15 minutes, then turn out onto a wire rack and leave to cool completely before slicing.

Lemon and Spice Tea with Bircher Finish

My wife and I make this morning 'kicker' quite often. We used to always spoon out the grated bits from the bottom of our mug and eat them – it's all good stuff – then my wife started stirring a spoonful of yoghurt into hers. And now I sometimes go further and mix in some oats and grated apple – for a quick-fix spicy Bircher.

Serves 2

2 cardamom pods
2cm piece of fresh ginger
2–3cm piece of fresh turmeric
Finely grated zest and juice of
  ½ lemon or lime, to taste
A twist of black pepper or a pinch
  of dried chilli flakes

Bircher extras

1 tbsp jumbo porridge oats
½ eating apple, coarsely grated
A splash of apple juice or
  kombucha
1 heaped tbsp natural yoghurt
  or kefir

Bash the cardamom pods once or twice with a rolling pin to crack them open and release the seeds, then crush the seeds with the rolling pin or using a pestle and mortar. Finely grated the ginger and turmeric.

Put the ginger, turmeric, cardamom, lemon or lime zest and pepper or chilli flakes into 2 mugs. Pour over enough boiling water to almost fill them and leave to infuse for 5 minutes. Add the lemon or lime juice to taste (you may prefer less than ½ lemon/lime).

Drink your cups of tea to the last swig or so.

Now, if you want to make the Bircher, empty the grated bits in the bottom of each cup into a small bowl.

Add the oats and grated apple to the bowl and pour on the apple juice or kombucha, to just cover everything. Stir and then leave for at least 10 minutes to allow the oats to soften. Stir in a spoonful of yoghurt or kefir and it's ready to eat.

Chocolate, Coffee and Turmeric Booster

Try swapping your usual morning coffee or tea with a cup of this. Or have both – this is great for a mid-morning boost instead of your second coffee. You can leave out the coffee for a caffeine-free version too. If I'm making this just for me, I still make enough for 2 servings, so I can have a chilled (or reheated) version the following day.

Serves 2

100ml milk (dairy or oat/nut milk)
100ml freshly boiled water
2–4 espresso shots of coffee
  (or 150ml coffee from a cafetière)
2 tbsp cacao powder
1 tsp ground turmeric
½ tsp ground cinnamon (optional)
1 tsp honey or sugar (optional)

Pour the milk into a small saucepan and heat gently until almost simmering, then add the boiling-hot water, along with the coffee, cacao powder, turmeric and cinnamon, if using.

Add a little honey or sugar, too, if you'd like a lightly sweetened version. Whisk until smooth, then pour into mugs and enjoy.

Chilled Version
Allow the drink to cool and then pour over two tumblers of ice to serve.

Six-packed Soups and Stoups

Soup is universal comfort food – a nourishing repository for good things, whatever the season. Whether it's a chunky, hearty winter warmer full of grains and pulses, a creamy seafood chowder or a cooling veg-packed gazpacho, it's hard not to feel better after a bowlful. And the great thing about soups is that they are so ready for a finishing touch or two: a dusting of spice, a spoonful of seeds or a trickle of oil-loosened pesto makes them doubly delicious and, of course, ups the plant count.

In this chapter, you'll find some simple classics, a few flavourful new creations that I hope you'll enjoy – and I've plant-packed some of my old faithfuls too, revamping them with a few tweaks and tricks so that they feel like they truly belong in a high-variety diet.

I've focused on vegetables, pulses and grains, forgoing meat and fish to show you just how much soupy supper you can get out of plants alone. These recipes all have at least six plants in them – many of them quite a few more – and are among the best examples of how easy it is to eat 30 plants a week. Most of them are vegan-friendly too, with an optional dollop of yoghurt, crème fraîche or cheese here and there, if you like.

You can, of course, add flavour and texture without adding dairy products: Black bean, corn and tomato soup (on page 65), for instance, uses lightly pickled red onion to zip it up at the end. And I'd definitely recommend trying the soaked-and-blitzed nuts technique to enrich soups. For example, for my Creamy roast cauli and cashew soup (on page 57), soaked cashew nuts are whizzed up with the roasted cauliflower for a smooth, silky texture.

While a lot of soups are traditionally finished with a glug of cream, instead you can trickle over a little of my Sunflower and oat cream (from page 220) for an equally luxurious finish. These simple additions can make a huge difference to your weekly plant tally.

I rarely try to make 'just-enough' soup, and all these recipes can be doubled-up, assuming you've got a big enough pan. Cooking too much for one meal means you've got a few bowlfuls for the rest of the week, or to go in the freezer. I sometimes reheat a portion and pour it into a Thermos to take with me when I'm out and about. When it comes to lunchtime, it's a joy to sit and enjoy a mug of leftover soup rather than a not-very-satisfying shop-bought sandwich.

You don't need anything else to make a meal of these soups – that's why I call some of them 'stoups' – my fun name for a soup that is really delivering as a stew. I won't begrudge you a slice of wholegrain toast, if that appeals. But thanks in large part to the grains and pulses I've already included, a generous portion of any of them is a lunch or supper in itself – beautifully balanced and super-sustaining.

Summer 'Salad' Stoup with Peas and Barley

Shroomami Stoup

Creamy Roast Cauli and Cashew Soup

Squash Mulligatawny

Nettle Soup with Pesto

Gazpacho

Black Bean, Corn and Tomato Soup

Super Six Standby Supper Stoup

Summer 'Salad' Stoup with Peas and Barley

This recipe is a great example of the versatility of summer greens that we often think of as 'salady' – the ingredients are very similar to the ones in my Big green summer salad on page 100. But here they appear in a 'stoup' (a cross between a stew and a soup), made hearty with spuds and grains. It may seem a bit weird to use lettuce and cucumber in a hot dish, but this recipe – with its lovely range of summer veg textures and flavours – shows just how much sense it can make…

Serves 4

75g pearl barley, rinsed
1 tbsp oil or fat
2 bunches of spring onions, trimmed and finely sliced
1 garlic clove, sliced
1 tsp English mustard
1 litre vegetable stock
200g small new potatoes, scrubbed and halved or quartered
400g freshly podded peas
2 Little Gem or Butterhead lettuces, roughly shredded
½ cucumber, peeled and cut into 1cm dice
A bunch of parsley, leaves picked and roughly chopped
A few sprigs of mint, leaves picked and roughly chopped
Sea salt and black pepper

If you have time, pre-soak the pearl barley in cold water for about 30 minutes, then drain.

Heat the oil or fat in a medium saucepan over a moderate heat. Add the spring onions and sizzle gently, stirring often, for about 5 minutes until soft but not coloured. Add the garlic and cook for a further 2 minutes.

In a jug, whisk the mustard into the stock to combine then pour into the soup pan and add the pearl barley. Bring to a simmer, then turn the heat down, so that the stock is just simmering. Cook for 20 minutes until the barley is almost tender, then add the potatoes. Simmer for another 10–15 minutes until the spuds are tender too.

Now add the peas, shredded lettuce and diced cucumber. Bring back to a simmer and cook gently for 3 minutes, until the lettuce is wilted and tender.

Taste to check the seasoning and tweak if necessary, then stir through most of the chopped herbs. Ladle the soup into warmed bowls and scatter over the remaining herbs to serve.

Swaps and Additions
You can add or swap in other summer veg such as broad beans and green beans – these will take a little longer to cook than the peas, so add them a few minutes before the lettuce and cucumber. And courgettes can go in instead of, or as well as, the cucumber.

Autumn/Winter Version
Use a couple of regular onions, finely sliced, instead of the spring onions; peeled winter spuds instead of new potatoes; frozen rather than fresh peas, or a 400g tin of beans; and kale, cabbage or other winter greens instead of the lettuce. That's a lot of swaps – but the method is just the same and it's still a fabulous soup.

Shroomami Stoup

A good mushroom soup has deep umami flavours that make it really satisfying. Here, these are enhanced by two cheeky ingredients I often use to give gravies a bit of a boost: red wine and coffee. You won't taste either – unless you overdo it. The other trick is to get as much colour on the mushrooms and other veg as possible at the start, as these 'browning flavours' lend depth and richness. Lentils add body and creaminess, making the soup substantial.

As a bonus, a simple tweak plus an extra blitz gives you a truly excellent vegan gravy – great, for example, with my Festive spiced stuffed squash (on page 176).

Serves 4

Oil or fat for cooking
350–400g open cap, portobello
   or chestnut mushrooms, sliced
   (or replace 100g with shiitake
   or oyster mushrooms)
3 large shallots, or 2 medium
   onions, finely chopped
1 large or 2 medium carrots,
   finely chopped
2 celery sticks (or a wedge of
   celeriac), finely diced
A few sprigs of thyme, leaves
   picked and roughly chopped
3 garlic cloves, finely chopped
100ml red wine
2 tbsp freshly made coffee
400g tin green lentils, drained
   and rinsed (or 200g cooked
   Puy or green lentils)
1 litre vegetable or chicken stock
A small bunch of parsley, leaves
   picked and roughly chopped
Sea salt and black pepper

To serve (optional)
50ml crème fraîche, or
   Sunflower and oat cream
   (page 220)
1–2 tbsp extra virgin olive or
   rapeseed oil

Heat a little oil or fat in a large, wide saucepan over a medium heat. Add the mushrooms and fry for 8–10 minutes or until deep golden brown. If they release any liquid, let it bubble away and keep frying until the mushrooms are nicely coloured, adding a little more oil or fat if needed.

Now add the shallots or onions, carrot(s), celery and thyme to the pan and sauté for 10 minutes or so until well coloured, even burnt in places – just a little. Add the garlic and sauté for a further minute (don't burn that!).

Add the wine and coffee and stir well, letting the liquid bubble and reduce a little. Tip in the lentils, pour in the stock and bring to a gentle simmer. Cook for 8–10 minutes or so, until all the veg are tender.

Using a stick blender, partially blitz the soup, so it thickens but still has plenty of texture. Or ladle half if it into a jug blender, blitz and then stir back into the rest. (Alternatively, you can blend the soup until smooth if you prefer.) Stir in three-quarters of the parsley. Taste to check the seasoning and add salt and/or pepper if needed.

Spoon the soup into warmed bowls and top each serving with a spoonful of crème fraîche or sunflower and oat cream, a trickle of extra virgin oil and a final sprinkling of chopped parsley.

Shroomami Vegan Gravy
Prepare the recipe as above, keeping it vegan by using a vegetable oil to fry the mushrooms and sticking to veg stock. Reduce the lentils to a scant 50g (or leave out altogether). Blitz until smooth, transfer to a pan, and reheat over a low heat. Stir in just enough hot veg stock to get a nice, pourable consistency; adjust the seasoning. Serve in a warmed jug whenever a vegan gravy is called for.

Creamy Roast Cauli and Cashew Soup

This is a deliciously creamy white soup, packed with lots of lovely alliums (leek, onion, garlic), which get roasted with the cauli. If you have time, leave the cashews to soak for a few hours to soften – they'll blend to a smoother finish. The garlic topping is a great addition and can be made ahead, but it's by no means essential. The soup is lovely on its own, or with a dollop of my Seven-plant pesto (on page 216).

Serves 4

100g cashew nuts
1.2–1.5 litres hot vegetable
  stock
1 large cauliflower (about 1.5kg),
  trimmed and cut into small
  florets, leaves kept
2 leeks, trimmed and cut into
  chunks
1 large onion, roughly chopped
3 celery sticks, roughly chopped
1 tsp cumin seeds
2 tbsp oil or melted fat
5 sprigs of thyme, leaves picked
Sea salt and black pepper

Garlic oil topping

3 tbsp extra virgin olive oil
2 garlic cloves, finely sliced
2 tbsp sunflower or pumpkin
  seeds (or a mix)
A pinch of dried chilli flakes

To finish

A small handful of chives, finely
  chopped, and/or parsley

Put the cashews into a bowl, pour on 1.2 litres hot stock and leave to soak for at least an hour.

Preheat the oven to 190°C/170°C Fan/Gas 5.

Put the cauliflower florets into a large roasting tray, along with their roughly chopped leaves (if they're in good nick). Add all the other veg and the cumin seeds. Add the oil or fat, season well with salt and pepper and toss the veg to coat lightly.

Transfer the roasting tray to the oven and roast for 20–25 minutes until all the veg are tender and golden.

In the meantime, make the topping. Put the extra virgin olive oil into a small saucepan with the garlic, seeds, chilli flakes and a pinch of salt. Place over a medium heat and heat gently for just a minute or two until the garlic starts to turn pale golden. Immediately take off the heat and pour the garlicky oil into a bowl. Leave to infuse until the soup is ready.

Scrape the contents of the roasting tray into a jug blender, add the thyme leaves and tip in the cashew nuts, along with their soaking liquor. Blitz until smooth. Return the soup to the saucepan and reheat gently, without boiling. (Or you can blitz the soup directly in a saucepan, using a stick blender, as you reheat it.) Either way, add a dash more stock to thin the soup a little if it seems too thick.

Ladle the soup into warmed bowls and top each serving with a trickle of the crispy garlic oil and a sprinkle of chopped chives and/or parsley.

Squash Mulligatawny

Mulligatawny is originally a soup from southern India, which traditionally uses chicken. This hearty vegetarian adaptation, with chunky pieces of squash, is very much in the 'stoup' category. Partnered with red lentils and turmeric, the squash conjures up a gorgeous deep orange colour, and with all the warming spicy flavours it is hard to resist. I like to top it with a generous dollop of raita flavoured with grated squash.

Serves 4–6

2 tbsp oil or fat
2 medium onions, sliced
2 leeks, trimmed and finely sliced
4 garlic cloves, sliced or grated
3–4 curry leaves (optional)
2 tsp medium curry powder
  or paste
½ tsp dried chilli flakes
3cm piece of fresh turmeric,
  grated (or 1 tsp ground)
4 cardamom pods, seeds
  extracted and lightly crushed
400g tin peeled plum tomatoes
1 small butternut squash or onion
  squash, or ½ medium Crown
  Prince, peeled and deseeded
  (about 500g prepared weight)
200g red lentils, rinsed
600ml vegetable stock
  (or water)
200ml coconut milk
Juice of 2 limes or 1 lemon,
  or to taste
Sea salt and black pepper

To serve (optional)
Raita with added grated squash
  (page 219, see swaps)

Heat the oil or fat in a medium saucepan over a medium heat. Add the onions and leeks, reduce the heat to low and cook for about 10 minutes, stirring regularly, until softened.

Add the garlic, stir well and cook for 1 minute, then add the curry leaves if using, curry powder or paste, chilli flakes, turmeric and crushed cardamom seeds. Cook over a low heat for a few minutes to release the spice flavours.

Now add the tinned tomatoes, crushing them with your hands as they go in (and picking out any stalky ends or bits of skin). Give the pan a good stir and season with salt and pepper. Cook gently for 10 minutes or until the liquid is reduced and thickened.

Meanwhile, roughly chop the squash into 4cm pieces, setting aside a small wedge to grate for the raita if serving.

Add the squash to the saucepan, stir and cook for 5 minutes, then add the lentils. Give the pan another good stir, then pour in the stock (or water). Partially cover the pan with the lid and simmer gently for around 20 minutes until the lentils are tender and the squash is soft.

Stir in the coconut milk and heat through. The mulligatawny will now be a deep, vibrant orange colour and have heaps of flavour. Taste to check the seasoning and add salt and/or pepper if needed. Remove from the heat and stir through lime or lemon juice to taste.

Ladle the mulligatawny into warmed bowls and serve, with a bowl of squash raita on the side if you like.

Nettle Soup with Pesto

This lovely, hearty soup is particularly fun to make in March and April when you have young nettles and the first wild garlic to play with. Use stout gloves to pick the nettles, gathering only the top crown of tender leaves from young plants that are not yet flowering. Then you can use everything, without stripping the leaves from the stalks. They will wilt quickly and blitz easily into the soup.

Serves 3–4

2 tbsp oil or fat
2 medium onions, finely sliced
3 celery sticks, sliced
A wedge of celeriac (about 100g), peeled and diced (optional)
1 heaped tsp fennel or caraway seeds (optional)
A couple of bay leaves
1 medium floury potato, scrubbed but not peeled and cut into 4cm pieces
1.2 litres vegetable stock
About 250g tender nettle tops, well washed (or 125g each spinach and nettles)
Sea salt and black pepper

To serve
Seven-plant pesto (page 216)

Heat the oil or fat in a large saucepan over a medium heat. Add the onions, celery, celeriac if using, fennel or caraway seeds if using, and the bay leaves. Give everything a good stir and season with some salt and pepper. Lower the heat and sweat gently for 8–10 minutes, stirring occasionally, until all the veg are tender.

Add the potato to the pan and stir well, then pour in the stock. Bring to a gentle simmer and cook for 10–12 minutes, or until the potato is just tender.

Now stir the nettle tops (and other greens if using) into the soup, and bring back to a simmer. They will quickly wilt down and should be tender after a couple of minutes simmering.

Take the pan off the heat and carefully blitz using a hand blender until you have a flecked, bright green soup. (If you don't have a hand blender, you can use a jug blender to blitz the soup, returning it to the warm pan to reheat gently over a very low heat.) Taste to check the seasoning and add salt and pepper if needed.

Divide the soup between warmed bowls and top each serving with a generous dollop of pesto. Serve immediately.

Swaps and Additions
Outside of the nettle season, you can replace them with watercress, or a combination of watercress and spinach for an equally delicious variation. The wedge of celeriac can be swapped with a medium carrot or parsnip. You can use a 400g tin of white beans, such as cannellini or butter beans to thicken the soup, instead of the potato, adding them with the nettles. And you can add a couple of handfuls of lemony sorrel to any version. A freshly poached egg is also a lovely way to finish to each serving, along with the plant-rich pesto.

Gazpacho

I've written and eaten many gazpacho recipes down the years, and I still love them. In my favourite latest version, I use white beans instead of bread to thicken the soup, so it's more wholesome, and serve it up with a garnish of all the soup veg, chopped, so it's like having a chunky salsa in the soup.

In the heat of the summer the garden and shops are full of sweet tomatoes. Earlier in the summer, before tomatoes are abundant, gooseberries can be used in just the same way, which may sound quirky but is delicious (see below). Use broad beans (fresh or frozen) instead of white beans, for a gorgeous green gazpacho.

Serves 4

1.5kg very ripe, large tomatoes

400g tin white beans, such as haricot, cannellini or butter beans (or chickpeas), drained and rinsed

½ cucumber, peeled and sliced

1 red pepper, cored, deseeded and cut into 2cm pieces

1 small red onion, chopped

50g almonds, roughly chopped (optional)

1 garlic clove (peeled)

1 tbsp balsamic vinegar (ideally apple balsamic)

80ml extra virgin olive oil

A few ice cubes (optional)

A small handful of basil and/or parsley, roughly chopped

6–8 chives, snipped

Sea salt and black pepper

Cut a little cross on the bottom of each tomato and place them all in a large bowl. Cover with boiling water and leave for a couple of minutes, then drain and peel off their skins.

Quarter and deseed the tomatoes, putting the seeds and clinging juicy bits into a sieve over a bowl. Put the tomato flesh into another bowl. Press the seedy bits in the sieve to extract the juice.

Put three-quarters of the tomatoes, beans, cucumber, red pepper, onion and almonds if using into a blender, setting aside the rest of each for serving. Add the garlic, sieved tomato juice, balsamic vinegar and 50ml of the extra virgin olive oil. Pour in 200ml cold water (or to speed up the chilling, use less water and add a few ice cubes). Season with a little salt and pepper and blitz until smooth.

Pour into a bowl, cover and chill in the fridge for 2–3 hours. Taste to check the seasoning and add salt and/or pepper if needed.

To prepare the garnish, in a bowl, slightly break up the rest of the beans with a fork. Roughly chop the retained tomato flesh and add to the beans with the rest of the cucumber, red pepper and onion, chopped almonds if using, chopped herbs and remaining 2 tbsp extra virgin olive oil. Toss to mix.

Ladle the chilled soup into bowls and top each portion with the salad garnish to serve.

Gooseberry Gazpacho

Replace the tomatoes with 1kg sweet, ripe gooseberries. Instead of white beans, use 200g cooked fresh or frozen broad beans, popped out of their skins (or stick with tinned white beans if broad beans are hard to come by). Prepare as above, blitzing the gooseberries whole and adding a sprig of mint to the blender. Make a similar garnish with chopped gooseberries and bashed broad beans, using shredded mint instead of basil or parsley.

Black Bean, Corn and Tomato Soup

A hearty but zingy tomato soup with crunchy corn and punchy lightly pickled red onions. It's great in summer with large lush ripe tomatoes, but also delicious in winter as a store-cupboard standby with a tin of good quality tinned toms. I much prefer tinned whole plum tomatoes to the chopped ones, which often seem watery.

The avocado and soured cream/yoghurt finish is optional, but it does add a lovely creaminess… and another plant!

Serves 4

Oil or fat for cooking
2 red onions, finely chopped
3 garlic cloves, finely chopped
1–2 medium-hot green chillies, such as jalapeño, deseeded and finely chopped
1 tsp ground cumin
4 tbsp tomato purée
A handful of coriander, stalks and leaves separated, finely chopped
400g ripe tomatoes, cored, deseeded and finely chopped, or a 400g tin peeled plum tomatoes
400g tin black beans or black-eyed beans, drained and rinsed
700ml vegetable stock
2 corn-on-the-cob, or 400g frozen sweetcorn
150g frozen peas (optional)
Juice of 1 lime
Sea salt and black pepper

Pickled red onion
1 small red onion, finely sliced
Finely grated zest and juice of 1 lime

To finish (optional)
4–6 tbsp soured cream or Greek-style yoghurt
1 ripe avocado, peeled, stoned and chunkily diced
A squeeze of lime or lemon juice

First, prepare the pickled red onion. Put the sliced onion into a bowl with the lime zest and juice and a pinch of salt. Scrunch it all together with your fingers until the onion turns pink then set aside to pickle while you make the soup.

Heat a little oil or fat in a saucepan over a medium-low heat, then add the onions and sauté for 6–8 minutes or until softened and lightly coloured. Add the garlic, green chilli(es), cumin and tomato purée and cook, stirring, for a minute or two. Toss in the chopped coriander stalks.

Now add the tomatoes (if using tinned tomatoes, crush them with your hands as they go in, picking out any stalky ends or bits of skin). Tip the black beans into the pan, pour in the stock and season with salt and pepper. Bring to the boil and simmer gently for 15–20 minutes until the tomatoes have broken down.

Meanwhile, if using fresh corn, slice the kernels off the cobs. Add the corn kernels (fresh or frozen) to the pan, along with the peas if using, and simmer for a further 5 minutes. Remove from the heat and add the lime juice, then taste to check the seasoning and adjust if necessary.

Ladle the soup into warmed bowls and top with a sprinkling of pickled red onion. Finish with a scattering of chopped coriander leaves, plus a little soured cream or yoghurt, avocado and a squeeze of lime or lemon juice if you like.

Swaps and Additions
Red kidney beans, carlin peas, cannellini beans, chickpeas and lentils are all great swaps for the black beans.
Also, you can make this hearty soup even more substantial by adding extra veg, according to the season: green or runner beans; diced courgettes or squash; and shredded greens such as kale or spinach.

Super Six Standby Supper Stoup

The idea here is to make a robust and tasty six-plant (minimum) stoup even when you think you haven't got the ingredients! More likely than not you'll have an onion and a couple of carrots to hand… and some peas and sweetcorn in the freezer. Plus a tin of beans (or lentils) sitting on the shelf. Once you get with the swing of my shopping and store-cupboard strategies, you will have all of the above and more! Just your own personal touch to add and you are already six plants in…

Serves 3–4

Oil or fat for cooking
2 medium onions, finely chopped
1 large or 2 medium carrots,
  chopped into bite-sized pieces
2 celery sticks (or a wedge of
  celeriac), chopped into bite-
  sized pieces
3 garlic cloves, finely chopped
1 litre hot vegetable or chicken
  stock (or water and 3–4 tsp
  miso paste)
400g tin lentils or beans, such
  as cannellini (or 150g frozen
  edamame or broad beans)
150g frozen peas
150g frozen sweetcorn
Up to around 100g leftover veg
  (if you have any), chopped
A few greens (if handy), shredded
Sea salt and black pepper

To finish (optional)
A handful of parsley or chives,
  roughly chopped (optional)
Extra virgin olive or rapeseed oil
  and toasted pumpkin seeds, or
  Seven-plant pesto (page 216)

Heat a little oil or fat in a large, wide saucepan over a medium heat. Add the onions, carrot(s) and celery (or celeriac) and sauté for 6–8 minutes until softened and golden. Add the garlic and sauté for another minute or two.

Pour in the stock (or just add the hot water at this point if using miso) and simmer gently for a few minutes until the veg are almost tender.

Tip in the lentils or beans, frozen veg and any leftover veg or greens you have mustered. Bring to a gentle simmer and cook for a further 3 minutes or so, until all the veg are tender. Take off the heat.

If using live miso paste, let the soup cool for a few moments before you add it, so the heat does not kill the beneficial bacteria. (Technically it should be just below 70°C when you stir the miso in, which is still piping hot.)

Taste the soup to check the seasoning and add salt and/or pepper if needed. Ladle into warmed bowls and sprinkle with the chopped herbs, if using. Finish with a trickle of extra virgin oil and a sprinkling of toasted pumpkin seeds, or a spoonful of pesto.

Six on the Stovetop Veg Suppers

This is one of my favourite chapters. It contains bubbling and flavourful Braised green beans with chickpeas and olives (page 73), a veg-rich dhal (on page 86), a glorious stir-fry (on page 76), a creamy-textured squash speltotto (on page 74) and a crisp Double and squeak (page 89) that can absorb all your leftover veg.

And, while the title is 'suppers', I think most of these lovely veggie 'mains' are great at any time of day. Mushrooms on toast, for instance, is a fine way to start the day (see page 85), in this case with gorgeous greens and olives muddled in, to really make a meal of it.

I have had a lot of fun here 'whole-ing up' some classics and family favourites, augmenting them with at least a couple of extra plants, often more, so that every recipe hits or exceeds the six-plant target. My take on the beautiful Sicilian dish caponata (on page 80), for example, uses courgettes, chickpeas and dried apricots as well as aubergines, celery and pine nuts. It tastes even better the next day, so try and save some for tomorrow's lunch.

There's a spin on a gribiche sauce too, made with hard-boiled eggs and punchy cornichons and capers, but also seaweed. (You'll find seaweed flakes scattered into the mushroom recipe too for a deep umami flavour and extra nutrients.) The gribiche is served with not one, but three wonderful charred veg. In fact, there's a fair bit of toasting, searing and charring going on through this chapter – always a fail-safe way to add flavour to plants.

Stovetop dishes are a great opportunity to add, swap and enhance, perusing the fridge, store-cupboard and spice rack as you go. Your pan is 'open', you can smell and stir as you cook, tasting a spoonful now and then to get a really good sense of what you are creating, and reaching for anything that will help to make it sing. With that in mind, there are plenty of swaps for you in this chapter. But trust your own instincts too, in finding even more plants to fling into your pot. Whenever you reach for it, you will soon be filling the kitchen with delicious smells and getting mouths watering.

Whether you're after something simple yet vibrant and nourishing, such as toasted walnut and fresh tomato pasta (see page 79), or a more multi-layered, spiced up offering like my Sichuan-style aubergine (on page 76) – which uses whole black beans, in addition to tofu, chilli paste and the famous mouth-tingling Sichuan pepper – there are plenty of super supper solutions for you here.

I want this chapter to become your first port of call when stomachs are rumbling at the end of the day, or any time of day.

Charred Veg with Seaweed Gribiche

Braised Green Beans with Chickpeas and Olives

Roast Squash and Kale Speltotto

Sichuan Aubergine with Tofu and Black Beans

Toasted Walnuts, Fresh Tomatoes and Pasta

Caponata with Chickpeas and Apricots

Beans, Greens, Pasta and Pesto

(More Than) Mushrooms on Toast

Very Veggie Double Dhal

Double and Squeak

Charred Veg with Seaweed Gribiche

This lovely recipe comes from our River Cottage Chef Tutor Chiara Tomasoni. Dried seaweed is a handy secret ingredient: it's not just a useful umami flavour booster, it's also packed full of plant nutrients. I suggest getting mixed seaweed flakes as they are so easy to use, but dried dulse and nori sheets are good all-rounders, and can be blitzed into flakes. Although seaweed is a great addition here, it's not essential, so omit if you can't find it.

The last of the purple sprouting overlaps with the first asparagus in late spring, but there are other veg you can grill – see my suggestions below.

Serves 4

A bunch of asparagus
200g purple sprouting or
  tenderstem broccoli
A bunch of spring onions,
  trimmed
1 tbsp vegetable oil
Flaky sea salt

Gribiche

4 medium eggs (at room
  temperature)
2 garlic cloves, finely grated
1 tsp Dijon mustard
Finely grated zest and juice of
  ½ lemon
100ml extra virgin olive oil
75g cornichons or gherkins,
  finely chopped
1 shallot or small onion,
  finely chopped
2 tbsp dried mixed seaweed
  flakes (or use nori or dulse)
2 tbsp capers, roughly chopped
A small bunch of parsley, leaves
  picked and finely chopped
½ small bunch of chives, finely
  chopped
Black pepper

To finish

½ lemon

Start by making the gribiche. Add the eggs to a pan of simmering water and cook for 8 minutes. Remove and tap to crack the shells then plunge into a bowl of cold water to cool quickly. Peel the cooled eggs, cut them in half and separate the whites from the yolks. Chop the egg whites and set aside.

Put the cooked egg yolks into a bowl with the garlic, mustard, lemon zest and juice. Whisk to combine and then trickle in the extra virgin olive oil in a thin, steady stream, whisking as you do so, to create a thick sauce – like a slightly grainy mayonnaise. Stir through the chopped cornichons or gherkins, shallot or onion, seaweed, capers, chopped egg white and herbs. Taste for seasoning, adding pepper (you won't need salt).

Massage the asparagus, broccoli and spring onions with the oil, using your fingertips, and then sprinkle with a little flaky salt.

You'll need to cook the veg in batches: heat a dry heavy-based frying pan or cast-iron griddle over a high heat until almost smoking. Add a layer of veg and grill, turning occasionally, until nicely charred on all sides (but still with a few green patches). Remove with a slotted spoon to a warmed serving platter. Repeat to char the rest of the veg.

Squeeze the juice from the lemon half over the charred veg and spoon half of the gribiche on top of them. Serve the rest of the gribiche in a bowl on the side for everyone to help themselves.

Swaps
There are plenty of other veg you can grill here: green beans (especially flat ones, such as Helda; sugar snap peas or mangetout; courgettes in lengthways slices; wedges of Little Gem lettuce; slices of fennel. For the gribiche, sauerkraut is a great alternative to the cornichons, or even better, use half of each. Finely chopped green olives and pickled green chillies are other good options here.

Braised Green Beans with Chickpeas and Olives

Braising green beans with tomatoes and other tasty things is popular throughout the Med, and I've been doing it for years with my home-grown French and runner beans. This version has lots going on, and is fantastic served as a starter or part of a mezze spread, with a dollop of yoghurt and a lemon wedge on the side. It is also great as a side to lamb, fish or roast chicken. It's lovely eaten soon after cooking, but arguably even better the next day. So, you can make it in advance and store it in the fridge for a day or two, removing it an hour or so before serving to bring it to room temperature.

Serves 4 as a side or starter, or 2 as a main

Oil or fat for cooking
1 large onion, finely chopped
2 garlic cloves, finely sliced
1 tbsp tomato purée
1 tsp paprika
1 tsp ground cumin
A pinch of dried chilli flakes
2 x 400g tins peeled plum tomatoes
300g green (French) beans, trimmed
400g tin chickpeas, drained and rinsed
100g pitted black olives, such as Kalamata
Sea salt and black pepper

To serve

4–5 tbsp natural yoghurt and/or 50g feta
A handful of parsley, mint or basil (or a mix), leaves picked and roughly chopped
A pinch of dried chilli flakes (optional)
Lemon wedges

Heat a splash of oil or knob of fat in a flameproof casserole or large saucepan over a medium heat. Add the onion with a pinch of salt and fry gently for at least 15 minutes, until very soft, golden and slightly caramelised – the more time you give the onion the better, as long as you don't burn it! Add a little more oil if needed during cooking.

Add the garlic, tomato purée, ground spices and chilli flakes. Cook, stirring, for a couple of minutes, taking care not to burn the garlic. Add the tinned tomatoes, crushing them with your hands as they go in and picking out any stalky ends or bits of skin. Add a splash of water to the empty tins to sloosh out the last of the juice; add this too.

Bring to a simmer and cook for about 15 minutes until the tomato sauce is reduced and thickened a little. Add the green beans, chickpeas and olives and simmer for a further 25 minutes until the beans are really tender.

Serve the braised beans warm or at room temperature. It's nice to bring them to the table with the yoghurt, herbs, chilli flakes if using, and lemon wedges in small bowls, so that everyone can serve themselves and dress their own plates.

Swaps and Additions
Instead of the green beans, use runner beans, trimmed of their stringy edges and cut into 5cm lengths. Or replace the beans with a couple of courgettes, halved lengthways and cut into 2cm slices on the diagonal. Swap the chickpeas for cannellini, kidney, aduki or butter beans if you like. You can also add 1 tbsp capers instead of, or as well as, the olives.

Roast Squash and Kale Speltotto

Spelt is an ancient grain with a nutty flavour and it's a great alternative to rice for a risotto – making it a 'speltotto'. This lovely autumnal version combines spelt with a tray of roast veg. It's enriched at the end with my blitzed 'cream' made from soaked oats and sunflower seeds.

Serves 4

200g wholegrain spelt or pearl
   barley
1 small or ½ large squash, such
   as butternut or Crown Prince
3 small red onions or large
   shallots
2 tbsp oil or fat for cooking
1.2 litres hot vegetable stock
1 garlic bulb
60g pumpkin and/or sunflower
   seeds
A fistful of kale leaves (about
   75g), coarse stalks removed,
   roughly chopped
A few sprigs of rosemary or sage
150ml Sunflower and oat cream
   (page 220)
A squeeze of lemon juice
A small bunch of chives,
   chopped (optional)
Extra virgin olive or rapeseed oil
   to trickle
Sea salt and black pepper

Put the spelt or barley into a bowl, pour on cold water to cover and leave to soak for at least 30 minutes, and up to 2 hours.

Preheat the oven to 190°C/170°C Fan/Gas 5. Cut the squash into wedges or chunks, trimming off the tough skin and removing the seeds as you do so. Cut the onions or shallots into thick slices or thin wedges. Pile the squash and onions into an ovenproof dish and toss with a little of the oil or fat, and some salt and pepper. Roast in the oven for about 15 minutes.

Meanwhile, rinse the soaked spelt or barley well, tip into a large saucepan and pour on the hot stock. Bring to the boil, reduce the heat to a gentle simmer and cook for 40–50 minutes until the grains are plump and tender with just a little bite.

In the meantime, break up the garlic bulb into individual cloves and bruise each one lightly, then peel; set aside.

After 15 minutes, take out the dish of squash and toss in the garlic cloves, pumpkin/sunflower seeds, kale and rosemary or sage. Add a dash more oil and seasoning, and toss well. Return to the oven for 15–20 minutes until all the veg are tender and the squash is lightly caramelised. Remove from the oven and set aside.

Once the spelt or barley is tender it may or may not have absorbed all the stock (depending on how long the spelt has been soaked, and its age). If the pan is almost dry, add a dash of hot water. If it is very wet still, pour off a little stock.

Stir in the sunflower and oat cream, with the lemon juice, two-thirds of the chives if using, and a trickle of extra virgin oil. Now tip all of the roast veg into the pan and stir through, allowing the squash to break up.

Mound the speltotto gently onto warmed plates or into shallow bowls, allowing it to spread out. Finish with a final trickle of olive oil and a scattering of chives, if you have some, over each serving.

Swaps and Additions
For a 'multigrainotto' double or triple your grains, using pot barley and/or wheat berries as well as spelt, soaking and cooking all the grains together.

Six on the Stovetop Veg Suppers

Sichuan Aubergine with Tofu and Black Beans

This is a take on mapo tofu, a popular dish from the Sichuan province of China. The key to it is a lovely chilli paste, made with fresh chillies (ideally the fleshy and not-too-hot kind), chilli flakes (which provide the real heat) and Sichuan peppercorns, which have a wonderful tingly character that carries the flavours of this aromatic dish a long way.

Serves 4

2 medium aubergines
400g packet firm ready-to-cook
  tofu
A bunch of spring onions,
  trimmed
2–3 tbsp oil or fat for cooking
400g tin black beans, drained
  and rinsed
Fine sea salt

Chilli paste
2 large (not-too-hot) red chillies,
  deseeded and roughly chopped
½ tsp sea salt
1 tsp dried chilli flakes
½ tsp Sichuan peppercorns
2 garlic cloves, grated
3cm piece of fresh ginger, grated
1 tbsp soy sauce
1 tbsp vegetable oil

Cut the aubergines into 2–3cm cubes, tip into a colander and sprinkle with a little salt, making sure each piece gets a good pinch. Leave to drain off the juices.

To make the red chilli paste, pound all the ingredients, except the soy sauce and oil, to a paste, using a pestle and mortar. (Or, you can bash them together on a large board with the end of a rolling pin, scraping them back into a pile in the middle with the knife every now and again.) When you have a vibrant, speckled, thick red paste, transfer it to a small bowl and stir in the soy sauce and oil until well combined.

If the tofu looks wet, wrap it in a tea towel and squeeze firmly from various angles, to soak up the excess water. Cut the tofu into 2–3cm cubes. Cut the white part of the spring onions into 2cm slices on the diagonal, saving some of the green part to finish.

Drain the aubergine, squeezing to remove excess liquid, and pat dry with kitchen paper. Heat 2 tbsp oil or fat in a wok or large, deep frying pan over a high heat. Add the aubergine cubes and stir-fry for 8–10 minutes until golden brown and tender, adding a little more oil or fat to the pan as needed.

Lower the heat slightly and add about half of the chilli paste. Cook, tossing and stirring for a minute and then add the black beans. Toss everything together, letting the flavours mingle, and adding a few splashes of water (up to 100ml) to loosen and create a sauce – crush a few of the beans as you go to help thicken this sauce.

Taste for seasoning, adding a little more of the chilli paste if you think it's not hot enough, and another splash of water if needed.

Now add the tofu and white spring onions, and stir through gently, using a wooden spoon so as not to break the tofu. Allow to bubble in the sauce for a couple of minutes to just heat through.

Meanwhile, finely slice the reserved green spring onion on the diagonal then scatter over the stir-fry. This is delicious on its own, but can also be enjoyed with brown rice or wholegrain noodles.

Toasted Walnuts, Fresh Tomatoes and Pasta

This is a lovely way to dish up some pasta shapes with richly toasted nuts, tangy fresh tomatoes and a handful of herbs – kind of like a deconstructed pesto.

Serves 4

100g walnuts
1 garlic clove, finely chopped
3 tbsp extra virgin olive oil
50g pitted black olives, such
  as Kalamata
1 tbsp capers
200g cherry tomatoes, halved
  or quartered if larger
200g wholewheat pasta shapes,
  such as casarecce, penne or
  conchiglie
A small bunch of chives or spring
  onions, trimmed and chopped
A small bunch of basil (or parsley,
  or a mix), roughly chopped, plus
  a few whole leaves to finish
A squeeze of lemon juice
50g Parmesan or Cheddar,
  shaved or grated (optional)
Sea salt and black pepper

Place a dry heavy-based frying pan over a medium heat. Add the walnuts and leave for a minute or so, then toss well and toast for 5–8 minutes, stirring or tossing occasionally, until fragrant and light golden brown. Watch carefully, as the nuts turn from golden to burnt in a moment.

As soon as the walnuts are done, tip them out into a mortar or onto a board. Bash the still-hot walnuts with the chopped garlic and some salt and pepper to crumbs, using the pestle or the end of a rolling pin. If you're pounding the nuts on a board, you'll need to scrape them back into a pile in the middle with the knife every now and again.

Tip the bashed garlicky walnuts into a bowl and add the extra virgin olive oil, olives, capers and cherry tomatoes. Toss well together.

Bring a large pan of water to the boil, add salt and then the pasta. Cook until *al dente* (tender but firm to the bite). Drain well and add straight to the bowl of walnuts and tomatoes.

Tip in the chopped chives or spring onions and the basil (and/or parsley). Add a squeeze of lemon juice and season with salt and pepper to taste. Toss well and divide between warmed serving bowls. Scatter over the Parmesan or Cheddar, if using, and a few fresh basil (or parsley) leaves to finish.

Swaps and Additions
Feel free to use hazelnuts, pecans or pine nuts instead of the walnuts. For a double carb version, add either a 400g tin butter beans (drained and rinsed), warming them through in a pan with a dash of olive oil and water; or 250g just-cooked new potatoes. Toss the beans or spuds through the pasta with the tomatoes and walnuts.

Caponata with Chickpeas and Apricots

Caponata is a gorgeous Sicilian sweet and sour dish with aubergine at its heart. I've included courgettes as well here, but you can use just aubergines if you prefer. I like the chunkiness the dried apricots lend, but feel free to introduce other dried fruits if you like. The chickpeas are not authentic, but they go very well with the flavours and textures, and make for a more substantial dish.

Caponata is classically served at room temperature and it keeps in the fridge for a few days, so it's a good one to make in advance.

Serves 4

2 medium aubergines
(about 500g in total)
2 medium courgettes (or use
another aubergine)
3 tbsp vegetable oil
1 onion, finely sliced
2 celery sticks, thinly sliced
2 garlic cloves, chopped
6 large plum or other ripe
tomatoes, peeled, deseeded
and chopped, or a 400g tin
peeled plum tomatoes
400g tin chickpeas, drained and
rinsed
2 tbsp balsamic vinegar
70g dried apricots (unsulphured),
roughly chopped
2 tbsp capers
60g pitted green olives, torn
in half
Sea salt and black pepper

To finish
50g pine nuts or pumpkin seeds,
toasted
A good handful of oregano leaves
(or basil or parsley)
A squeeze of lemon juice
Extra virgin olive oil to trickle

Cut the aubergines into 2–3cm cubes, tip into a colander and sprinkle with 2 tsp salt. Toss well and then leave to draw out the juices for about an hour. Cut the courgettes into similar-sized cubes; set aside.

About halfway through the aubergine salting time, heat 1 tbsp of the oil in a large saucepan over a fairly low heat. Add the onion and celery and fry for about 10 minutes until tender and golden. Toss in the garlic and cook for a further 2 minutes until fragrant.

Tip in the tomatoes (crushing tinned ones with your hands as they go in and picking out any stalky ends or bits of skin). Simmer for 10–15 minutes to reduce a little. Add the chickpeas, balsamic vinegar, dried apricots, capers and olives and simmer for another 10 minutes, stirring often. Remove from the heat.

Rinse the aubergines and pat dry with kitchen paper. Heat a little more oil in a large frying pan over a medium-high heat. When hot, add the aubergine cubes and fry for about 5–10 minutes, stirring occasionally, until golden and tender. Remove with a slotted spoon and drain on kitchen paper, then tip into the tomato mixture.

Add a little more oil to the pan and fry the courgettes in the same way, then drain and add to the aubergine and tomato mixture.

Bring back to a simmer and cook for another 10–15 minutes, stirring occasionally, until everything is well combined, reduced and thickened. Season with salt and pepper to taste.

Leave the caponata to cool to room temperature if you have time, or serve it hot if you prefer. Sprinkle with the toasted pine nuts or pumpkin seeds, oregano (or other herb) leaves, a squeeze of lemon and a trickle of extra virgin olive oil to finish.

Beans, Greens, Pasta and Pesto

Here's a fun way to use a multi-plant pesto. Wholegrain pasta and a tin of beans give you plenty of plant energy and fibre, plus two pleasingly different textures. Fresh greens, beans and leaves add crunch and yet more plant goodness. Clearly this is an idea to play around with (see my suggestions below).

Serves 4–5

3–4 tbsp Seven-plant pesto (page 216)
200g wholewheat pasta shapes, such as macaroni or rigatoni
150g green (French) beans, trimmed and halved
100g kale, spring greens, cavolo nero or spinach, coarse stalks removed, coarsely shredded
2 x 400g tins white beans, such as cannellini or butter beans, drained and rinsed
Sea salt and black pepper

To serve
Finely grated Parmesan, Cheddar or a vegetarian alternative (optional)
Extra virgin olive or rapeseed oil to trickle

Have your pesto made and ready to use.

Bring a large pan of water to the boil and add salt. You're going to add the pasta first, then the green beans. So, note the cooking time of the pasta as it goes in and add the green beans and kale about 4 minutes before the pasta will be done. Add the tinned beans for the last minute.

When the pasta and veg are done, scoop out and reserve half a mugful of the cooking water, then drain the pasta and veg and return to the hot pan.

Add 3–4 tbsp of the pesto and gently stir through the pasta and veg, trickling in a little of the hot pasta cooking water as you go, to help everything emulsify together.

Taste to check the seasoning and add salt and/or pepper if needed. Serve straight away in warmed bowls, with a twist of black pepper on top, a sprinkling of cheese if you like, and a final trickle of extra virgin oil.

Swaps and Additions
Swap the green beans for broccoli (or double up if you like). Cut into small florets, cutting the stalk into chunky dice; add to the pan 4 minutes before the pasta will be done. Frozen edamame beans or peas (or both) can be used instead, or as well as, the tinned beans.
Or you can go double carbs here by adding 200g small new potatoes: cook in lightly salted water until just tender, drain and thickly slice then add to the pasta with the tinned beans.

Six on the Stovetop Veg Suppers

(More than) Mushrooms on Toast

Mushrooms on toast is one of life's great pleasures, and the capers, olives and optional seaweed flakes give this a lovely umami booster. Going for at least two different mushroom varieties makes for a more interesting flavour and texture. A poached or fried egg (or two) alongside is a welcome extra treat.

Serves 2 as a main

200g chestnut or portobello
  mushrooms (or any mushrooms
  in season)
100g fresh oyster or shiitake
  mushrooms
Oil or fat for cooking
1 medium onion, finely sliced
2 garlic cloves, finely chopped
  or grated
2 tsp dried seaweed flakes
  (optional)
A sprig of thyme, leaves picked
  (optional)
A handful of olives, pitted and
  roughly chopped
1 tbsp capers
100g baby spinach leaves
A handful of parsley, leaves
  picked and finely chopped
Sea salt and black pepper

To serve
2–4 slices of wholemeal bread
2–4 poached or fried eggs
  (optional)

Cut the large mushrooms into thick slices; halve or quarter smaller ones. Place a large frying pan over a high heat. When hot, add 2 tbsp oil or a good knob of fat.

Now tip in all of the mushrooms and fry for 7–10 minutes, stirring regularly, until golden and crisp all over, seasoning with salt and pepper halfway through cooking. Scoop the mushrooms out of the pan onto a plate.

Add a little more oil or fat to the pan and turn down the heat to medium. Toss in the onion and sauté for 5–8 minutes until soft and lightly caramelised. Add a splash of water to the pan, stir through the garlic and seaweed flakes if using, and cook for another couple of minutes.

Now add the mushrooms back to the pan, along with the thyme if using, olives, capers and baby spinach. Cook briefly, tossing everything together, until the spinach is wilted. Stir through the chopped parsley with a few grinds of black pepper. Taste to check the seasoning and adjust if necessary.

Meanwhile, toast the bread. Lay a slice or two on each warmed plated and pile the mushrooms and spinach on top. Place the egg(s), if serving, alongside.

Very Veggie Double Dhal

Having a good dhal recipe up your sleeve is a great thing. And having a pot on the go for a few days, to put alongside other things (including sausages and fried eggs!) is very handy. This one is packed full of plants, with lovely spices and veg boosting a double dose of lentils. I like to serve it with a creamy raita, flavoured with toasted coconut.

Serves 4–6

200g red lentils

2 tbsp vegetable or coconut oil

2 medium onions, finely chopped

2 garlic cloves, finely grated or crushed

3–4cm piece of fresh ginger, grated

3cm piece of fresh turmeric, grated, or 1 tsp ground

2 tsp ground coriander

1 tsp ground cumin

2 large carrots, scrubbed and coarsely grated

400g tin peeled plum tomatoes

400g tin Puy, green or brown lentils, or 200g pre-cooked lentils

200g tin coconut milk (optional)

Finely grated zest and juice of 1 lime or ½ lemon, or to taste

Sea salt and black pepper

To serve (optional)

Raita or coconut raita (page 219)

Rinse the red lentils thoroughly and leave to soak in cold water while you start the dhal.

Heat the oil in a large saucepan over a medium-low heat. Add the onions and fry for 10 minutes until soft and lightly caramelised. Stir in the garlic, ginger, turmeric, coriander and cumin and fry gently for a couple of minutes, making sure the garlic doesn't burn.

Tip in the grated carrots and stir to mix with the spices. Now add the tinned tomatoes, crushing them with your hands as they go in and picking out any stalky ends or bits of skin. Bring to a brisk simmer and cook, uncovered, for 10 minutes or so, to reduce and thicken the sauce.

Give the red lentils a final rinse, then add to the pan along with 200ml water. Stir and bring back to a simmer. Cook, uncovered, stirring often, for 20–30 minutes, until the lentils are completely tender and the dhal is thick, stirring with a whisk towards the end to help break down the lentils.

Stir the tinned lentils through the dhal, along with the coconut milk if using. Let bubble for 5 minutes then turn off the heat and stir in lime or lemon juice to taste. Leave to sit for 10 minutes – the dhal will thicken up on standing. Taste to check the seasoning, adding salt and pepper and more citrus juice if needed.

Serve the dhal with the raita (if you've made it) and finish with a scattering of lime or lemon zest. A simple green salad on the side is all you need, this is really a meal in itself.

Swaps
Use grated beetroot instead of carrots for a lovely purple dhal. Parsnips and celeriac are other suitable alternatives.

Double and Squeak

This is, of course, a leftovers classic and it's such a lovely one that if you're having mash or boiled potatoes for supper it is worth cooking extra so you can enjoy a bubble and squeak the following day. It's a great fridge-clearer too, using up any veggie leftovers and leafy greens. Be as creative as you like – just make sure you've got a good ratio of mashed potato and beans so it binds together.

Serves 3–4

Oil or fat for cooking
1 large onion or large leek, thinly sliced
1–2 garlic cloves, finely chopped
A few sprigs of rosemary or thyme, leaves picked and chopped (optional)
½ tsp cumin seeds, or 1–2 tsp curry powder or other favoured spice blend (optional)
About 100g leftover cooked roots, such as celeriac, parsnips or Jerusalem artichokes, roughly chopped, or raw roots, grated
About 200g cooked potatoes or cold mashed potato
400g tin butter beans, drained and rinsed
About 100g cooked greens, such as kale, cabbage, Brussels sprouts and/or broccoli, roughly chopped or shredded
About 100g frozen peas or edamame beans
A handful of parsley and/or chives, chopped (optional)
Sea salt and black pepper

To serve (optional)
Poached or fried eggs
Pickle or kraut (any of those on pages 223–30)

Heat a little oil or fat in a non-stick medium frying pan over a medium heat. Add the onion or leek, with a pinch of salt and some pepper, and fry gently for about 10 minutes until softened and starting to colour.

Stir in the garlic, chopped rosemary or thyme if including, and cumin seeds or other spice if using. Cook, stirring, for a minute or two. If using grated raw roots, add these now and cook for an extra few minutes.

Tip the potatoes into the pan along with the beans and crush them roughly with a fork or masher, but keep the texture quite chunky (unless you're using mash). Fry for a few minutes, then add all the other veg (including any cooked roots), along with the chopped parsley and/or chives if using. Mix well, then press the whole lot down with the back of a spoon to compress together a little.

Now leave to cook for several minutes, to form a good golden-brown crust on the base. It's tempting to move the veg 'cake' but try not to: those burnt surfaces on the veg are what makes a bubble and squeak sing!

Once you have a nice crust, turn the veg over to brown and crisp up the other side. There's no need to flip the whole 'cake' in one go; you'll find it easier do it in quarters or wedges. Cook on the other side for several minutes until it is golden brown and crispy.

Cut the bubble and squeak into wedges and serve with a poached or fried egg on the side if you like. Any of my pickles or krauts would be a great accompaniment, too.

Magnificent Seven Salads

I hope there are few cooks, or indeed, eaters, left in the land who think of 'salads' as languishing at the duller end of the food spectrum. For me, salads play a vital role in adding a huge range of textures and flavours to the meals I make at home, and I absolutely love them. So much of the joy they bring naturally comes from plants. However, that doesn't mean we can't find opportunities to get even more plants into these colourful dishes.

Salads needn't be 'lite' and they're not just for summer: a hearty, well-dressed salad can be a great meal even in the depths of winter, either as a stand-alone or as a crucial side dish alongside a hearty stew or pie. That said, I'll embrace the salad mainstays of the warmer months wholeheartedly. I love a bowl of crisp, fresh lettuce, generously coated in a winning combination of oil, vinegar and mustard, inviting you to dive in as it sits in the centre of the table. But why stop there? In my Big green summer salad (on page 100) you'll find lovely lettuce rubbing shoulders with new potatoes, broad beans, peas, spring onions and herbs. It's a personal favourite and an excellent addition to your summer-long repertoire.

Beyond that, I've created a selection of salads brimming with textures and flavours to take you right through the year, on a bustling, rainbow-hued tour of plant-packed possibilities.

My fruit-laden, summer-into-autumn fruity 'Greek' salad (on page 94), with its plums, olives and lentils, is a fresh take on another old favourite. And Festive cabbage and clementine salad (on page 108) is pitch-perfect when you fancy something crisp, tangy and juicy to offset some of the richness of the season's feasting.

You'll discover a plethora of new ideas here, including some unexpected raw veg combos. Take, for example, my Dressed raw kale and squash (on page 106), in which shavings of uncooked squash make for a toothsome combination with massaged kale and a creamy, nutty dressing.

You'll also find classic dishes with a punchy plant-based twist, like my Purple panzanella (on page 98), which boosts the Italian bread-and-tomatoes classic with beetroot and plums. The result is a symphony of complementary tastes and textures – sweet, earthy and sharp; rooty, fruity and juicy – and it's as visually appealing as it is delicious!

Perhaps more than any other chapter, this one is ripe for experimentation. I've generally omitted meat and fish in favour of more vegetables, grains, nuts and seeds. However, by all means incorporate tinned or fresh fish here and there, or slices and shards of leftover meats, cold or hot, to suit your tastes and preferences.

In other words, I hope you'll use these recipes as inspiration for your own super-salady combinations. I've suggested a few specific swaps and variations, to guide you and get your ideas popping, but don't feel obliged to follow them word for word, or indeed, plant for plant. There are plenty of plants to play with, and few places more pleasing to put them than in a salad.

Herby Bean and Celery Salad

Fruity 'Greek' Salad with Lentils

Nutty Cauliflower and Leeks

Purple Panzanella

Big Green Summer Salad

Radicchio and Friends

Nutty Autumn Slaw

Dressed Raw Kale and Squash

Festive Cabbage and Clementine Salad

Herby Bean and Celery Salad

Here's a great store-cupboard salad, championing tinned beans. I like to use two different varieties of white beans, but really you can mix up the pulses as much as you like. I usually have some celery in the fridge, but a fennel bulb or even a chunk of cucumber would be a decent option. Go big on the fresh herbs if you can. If you have a vinaigrette standing by in the fridge, feel free to use it instead of the lemony dressing, although this is particularly good here.

Serves 2–3 as a light lunch, or 5–6 as a starter or side

400g tin butter beans, drained and rinsed

400g tin cannellini beans, drained and rinsed

3–4 inner, tender celery sticks, finely sliced

A small bunch of spring onions, trimmed (or a good handful of chives), finely sliced

A bunch of parsley, leaves picked and roughly chopped

A few mint, basil or lovage leaves, roughly chopped (optional)

Flaky sea salt and black pepper

Dressing

3 tbsp extra virgin olive oil

Finely grated zest and juice of ½ lemon, or more to taste

1 heaped tsp Dijon mustard

Tip all the beans into a large bowl and add the celery, spring onions and chopped herbs.

To make the dressing, in a small bowl, whisk together the extra virgin olive oil, lemon zest and juice, mustard and some salt and pepper. Or shake all the ingredients together in a screw-topped jar to emulsify.

Pour the dressing over the salad and toss well, making sure everything is well coated in the dressing. Taste to check the seasoning and adjust as necessary, with more lemon juice, salt and pepper as needed.

Leave the salad to mingle for 10 minutes or so, then tumble together again, and serve.

Swaps and Additions

Use a 400g tin of chickpeas instead of beans; large 'queen chickpeas' are particularly good. Or swap with a 400g tin of Puy, green or brown lentils. Switch the celery with a fennel bulb or ⅓–½ cucumber if you like. This salad also makes a great base or accompaniment for leftover cold meat, especially chicken or pork, or even sausages: tear or cut up and toss through the salad or serve alongside. It's also brilliant with tinned sardines or tinned or smoked mackerel.

Fruity 'Greek' Salad with Lentils

I'm not sure how much Greek is left in this salad, but the classic version was the starting point. I think California might have got a look in too, with the added fruit. My preference is for ripe plums, but peaches are also good alongside the feta and tomatoes. I've also tried it with watermelon, which works surprisingly well.

Serves 4

½ small red onion, finely sliced
1 ½ tbsp red wine vinegar or apple cider vinegar (ideally raw)
4 large plums (or 6 smaller ones), halved and stoned
½ cucumber, peeled if the skin is tough
2 large ripe tomatoes, or 200g cherry tomatoes
½ x 400g tin Puy, brown or green lentils, drained and rinsed, or about 100g pre-cooked lentils
A handful of Kalamata or green olives, halved and pitted
A small bunch of basil (or parsley), leaves picked
4 tbsp extra virgin olive oil
150g feta, drained
Sea salt and black pepper

Put the red onion into a small bowl with the vinegar and give it a good scrunch with your fingers so the onion pickles a little and turns pink.

Slice the plums into wedges and put into a large bowl. Cut the cucumber and tomatoes into roughly 2cm chunks, or halve cherry tomatoes, and add to the bowl. Sprinkle with a good pinch of salt and toss lightly. Leave to macerate for at least 15 minutes, or up to an hour (the salt will draws out juices, which go into the dressing).

Add the red onion and its soaking vinegar to the macerated fruit, along with the lentils, olives, most of the basil (or parsley) and 3 tbsp extra virgin olive oil. Add a generous grinding of pepper and toss everything together well. Leave for 10 minutes or so to mingle, then toss again.

Pile the salad onto a serving platter and crumble the feta over the top. Trickle with the remaining extra virgin olive oil, scatter over the rest of the basil (or parsley) and serve.

Swaps and Additions
Use cannellini, flageolet or butter beans, or chickpeas, in place of lentils. Peaches, nectarines and watermelon are all great swaps for plums when they are in season.

Nutty Cauliflower and Leeks

Here's a great-looking salad, beautifully balancing cooked and raw, with lovely contrasts between the crunchy caramelised cauli, sweet leeks, toasted nuts and tangy apple. It is delicious served straight away – slightly warm or at room temperature – but it's also good the next day, when the dressing and veg have mingled. So, you could make it ahead, keep it in the fridge, then bring it to room temperature to serve.

Serves 4

1 medium-small cauliflower (700g)
2 medium leeks, (about 300g in total), trimmed and washed
Oil or fat for cooking
1 crisp, tart eating apple, such as Cox, Russet or Braeburn
75g hazelnuts or walnuts, toasted and lightly bashed
A bunch of parsley, leaves picked and roughly torn

Dressing
Finely grated zest and juice of ½ lemon (or more to taste)
½ garlic clove, finely grated or crushed
50ml olive oil (or a little more to taste)
Sea salt and black pepper

Remove any leaves from the cauli, slice them fairly finely and set aside. Cut your cauli into quarters, through the stem, then cut each quarter into 2 or 3 wedges, depending on the size of the cauli. Chop any small bits of cauli that detach and keep with the leaves.

Cut the leeks on the diagonal into 1cm thick slices and set aside.

To make the dressing, whisk the ingredients together in a small bowl or shake in a screw-topped jar to combine, seasoning with salt and pepper to taste.

Place a large heavy-based sauté pan over a high heat and add just enough oil (or melt enough fat) to lightly coat the base. You will need to cook the cauli wedges in batches. Add a single layer to the pan and sauté until golden, and caramelised at the edges. Transfer to a bowl, using a slotted spoon, and add a tiny trickle more oil (or a little fat) before cooking the next batch.

When the cauli is all done, add a little more oil or fat to the pan, then toss in the leeks. Let them sizzle for a minute then lower the heat and sweat for 5 minutes or so, turning occasionally, until they are softening. Add the saved chopped cauliflower bits and leaves and cook for a further 2–3 minutes until the leeks are tender and the cauli bits are *al dente* (tender but firm to the bite). Add to the bowl with the cauliflower wedges.

Quarter, core and chop the apple into 1–2cm pieces. Add to the salad with the toasted nuts, parsley and the dressing. Toss together well. Taste to check the seasoning, adding salt and pepper as needed, plus a squeeze more lemon juice and a dash more oil if you like. Serve at once, on a platter or individual plates.

Swaps and Additions
This dish also works brilliantly if you replace the cauliflower with wedges of a tight-headed cabbage, such as Hispi.
You can also use thin wedges of onion or shallot instead of the leeks.
As well as, or instead of, the hazelnuts/walnuts, try adding some crumbled cooked chestnuts to the pan after sautéeing the leeks, cooking them for a few minutes until browned.

Purple Panzanella

This deep purple version of the classic Italian ripe tomato and stale bread salad is striking to look at and delicious to eat. Do give yourself a bit of time to make this, so the fruit and veg can macerate and release their juices to be soaked up by the bread. If you can find small young summer beetroot, grate them raw. Otherwise steam them for 20 minutes or so; or use pre-cooked beetroot.

Serves 4

2–3 beetroot, raw if baby beets, otherwise cooked, peeled (350–400g prepared weight)
1 red onion, thinly sliced
3 tbsp olive or rapeseed oil
2 tbsp balsamic or red wine vinegar
250g plums, halved and stoned
250g cherry tomatoes, quartered
150g slightly stale sourdough (ideally wholegrain) or brown bread
2 tbsp black olives, pitted
Sea salt and black pepper

To finish
12 basil leaves (purple if you can find it!)
Extra virgin olive oil

Coarsely grate the beetroot and place in a large bowl with the sliced onion. Add the oil, vinegar and some salt and pepper and toss well to combine.

Cut the plums into thick wedges then add to the bowl with the cherry tomatoes and toss lightly. Leave the salad to macerate for up to an hour, turning gently every 15–20 minutes to help the juices run – you want quite a bit of liquid so that it can soak into the bread.

Tear the sourdough roughly into small chunks and add to the bowl with the olives. Toss everything together and leave for at least another 10 minutes then toss again.

To serve, scatter some basil leaves over the salad and finish with a trickle of your best olive oil.

Swaps and Additions
Use grated or thinly shaved carrots instead of, or as well as, the beetroot. If you are a fan of radicchio, with its bitter notes and crunchy leaf, add ½ head, roughly shredded, at the start with the beetroot and onion. If you pick young beetroot yourself, add the tender young purple-veined leaves too: remove the tougher stalks, tear up the larger leaves, but keep the smaller leaves whole. Toss through the salad just before serving.

Big Green Summer Salad

This is rather like a niçoise without the fish or hard-boiled egg but with added peas and extra beans instead. The fish and egg are, of course, optional extras that will make a feast of it, albeit no longer vegan (see below). I also love this as a side to a roast chicken, eaten outside in the summer.

Don't be stressed about the exact quantities of veg here – it's just generous amounts of everything. A good vinaigrette is a handy thing to have in the fridge, so I've made more than you'll need for this salad.

Serves 2

About 150g cooked baby new potatoes (skin on)
About 100g cooked broad beans or edamame beans (frozen is fine)
About 100g cooked green (French) beans
About 100g cooked peas (frozen is fine)
A small bunch of spring onions, trimmed and sliced on the diagonal into 5mm–1cm slices
A handful of pea shoots (optional)
A small bunch of parsley, leaves picked
1–2 tsp capers (if you like them)
2 Little Gem or 1 Cos lettuce
1 Butterhead or other soft lettuce
1–2 handfuls of sorrel (optional)
A few sprigs of mint or basil, roughly chopped

Vinaigrette

2 tsp Dijon mustard (or 1 tsp English mustard)
1 scant tsp runny honey
4 tbsp apple cider vinegar (ideally raw) or wine vinegar
100ml extra virgin rapeseed or sunflower oil
100ml extra virgin olive oil
Sea salt and black pepper

First make the vinaigrette: shake all the ingredients together in a screw-topped jar to combine or whisk in a small bowl, seasoning with salt and pepper to taste. Either way, shake/whisk until well blended and creamy. And be ready to mix again thoroughly just before dressing the salad.

In a large salad bowl, combine the potatoes, beans and peas with the spring onions, pea shoots if using, parsley, and capers if using. Add 2 tbsp of the vinaigrette and toss together gently. (If you do this while the veg are still warm from cooking, they will mingle nicely with the dressing.)

Separate the lettuce into leaves. Just before serving, gently toss the lettuce leaves, sorrel if using, and chopped mint or basil with the dressed veg, adding another trickle of vinaigrette so everything is lightly dressed.

Keep the rest of the dressing in a sealed jar in the fridge and use within a couple of weeks.

Swaps and Additions
You can make this into even more of a main course by tossing in a 400g tin of butter beans (drained and rinsed) with the spuds and veg. Or you can go full niçoise with tinned fish and hard-boiled eggs. I would recommend tinned or smoked mackerel as a much more sustainable (and just as delicious) choice than tuna… plus a few anchovies for extra kick.

Radicchio and Friends

Radicchio is a bitter leaf that needs a little help to balance out its flavours: sweetness, acidity and a little heat are the way to go. The triple fruit addition of citrus, raisins and apple, plus the beetroot, chilli and beans, makes this a hearty, zesty and earthy salad that's perfect served on its own as a starter or alongside the Slow-roast Merguez spiced shoulder of lamb on page 140.

Serves 2 as a light lunch, or 4 as a side or starter

50g raisins
2 tbsp apple cider vinegar
  (ideally raw) or wine vinegar
1 radicchio
2 cooked medium beetroot,
  peeled
1 medium eating apple
400g tin black beans, drained
  and rinsed
2 medium oranges
1 tsp cumin seeds
3 tbsp extra virgin olive oil
½ tsp dried chilli flakes
Sea salt and black pepper

Put the raisins into a small bowl, pour on the vinegar and leave to soak for at least an hour.

Cut the radicchio into wedges, unfurling the leaves into wide ribbons. Place in a large salad bowl. Halve the beetroot, thinly slice into half-rounds and add to the radicchio. Quarter, core and thinly slice the apple and add to the bowl, with the black beans.

Finely grate the zest from the oranges and add it to the salad. Slice the top and bottom off the oranges, then stand upright on a board and slice off the peel from top to bottom, using a sharp knife, to expose the juicy flesh. Trim off any pith you've missed. Now turn the orange on its side and slice into rounds. (Or you can slice out the segments between the membranes, but you'll be missing some good fibre!)

Drop the orange slices (or segments) into the salad bowl and tip in any juice from the board.

Toast the cumin seeds in a small dry frying pan over a medium-high heat for a couple of minutes until fragrant and starting to pop. Let them cool, then crush lightly using a pestle and mortar, or on a board.

Add the toasted cumin to the bowl along with the raisins and their vinegar, the extra virgin olive oil and chilli flakes, a pinch of salt and a twist of pepper. Toss everything together and leave to mingle for 10 minutes or so. Toss once more, then serve on a platter or in individual bowls.

Swaps
Instead of radicchio, you can use other bitter leaves such as frisée or chicory. And/or swap cooked beetroot for raw carrot or celeriac.
You can also replace the oranges with 1 pink grapefruit or 3 blood oranges and swap the raisins for chopped prunes or dried apricots (unsulphured). And, of course, the black beans can be switched with another bean.

Magnificent Seven Salads

Nutty Autumn Slaw

A lovely crisp salad that's quick to pull together from the best autumn/winter leaves, fruits and nuts. It's a great side to serve alongside grilled or roast meats.

Serves 4 as a side

50g hazelnuts
1 tsp caraway seeds
½ white cabbage, finely
    shredded (250–300g)
2 medium carrots, scrubbed or
    peeled and grated
2 celery sticks, finely sliced
2 eating apples
Finely grated zest and juice of
    1 lemon
3 tbsp extra virgin rapeseed oil
Sea salt and black pepper

Toast the hazelnuts in a small dry frying pan over a medium-high heat for a few minutes until lightly coloured and fragrant then tip out onto a plate to cool.

Add the caraway seeds to the empty pan and toast for a minute or two until fragrant and starting to pop. Let cool, then crush lightly using a pestle and mortar, or on a board.

Give the toasted hazelnuts a bit of a bash too – just to break them up a little.

Tip the shredded cabbage into a large bowl and add the grated carrots and sliced celery. Quarter and core the apples, then slice thinly and add to the bowl, along with the lemon zest and juice. Toss to mix.

Add the toasted caraway seeds to the salad. Trickle over the rapeseed oil and season with a generous pinch of salt and a few twists of pepper. Give the salad a final toss and taste to check the seasoning. Transfer to a serving platter and scatter over the toasted nuts before serving.

Swaps and Additions
You can use red cabbage instead of white, parsnips instead of carrots, grated celeriac instead of sliced celery and pears instead of apples. You can also add cucumber and/or fennel, thinly sliced, if you have either. If you have some Dukka (page 209) to hand, you can use this instead of the hazelnuts. Or toast any other nuts and/or seeds you happen to have and use instead of, or as well as, the hazelnuts.

Dressed Raw Kale and Squash

Massaging raw kale with lemon juice (or cider vinegar) and a pinch of salt, then leaving it to macerate for a while tenderises it almost as though it's been cooked. It makes a great base for a salad. Here I've combined the softened kale with (equally surprising) raw squash, very thinly sliced. Tossed with toasted nuts and seeds and Ajo blanco – a creamy dressing based on the classic Spanish almond soup – it makes for a quirky but very pleasing salad.

Serves 4

40g raisins
2 tbsp apple cider vinegar
 (ideally raw) or wine vinegar
150g wedge of squash, such
 as butternut, onion or Crown
 Prince
100g kale leaves, stripped of their
 thick stalks (prepared weight)
50g blanched hazelnuts or
 almonds
30g sunflower or pumpkin seeds
 (or a mix)
1 tsp dried chilli flakes
½ quantity Ajo blanco dressing
 (page 221)
Lemon juice to taste (optional)
Sea salt and black pepper

To assemble

4 slices of wholegrain sourdough
Extra virgin olive oil to trickle

Put the raisins into a small bowl, pour on the vinegar and 2 tbsp freshly boiled water and leave to soak for at least an hour.

Cut away the skin from the squash and slice the flesh into very thin shavings, using a mandoline or veg peeler if you like. Slice or tear the kale leaves into thick ribbons, 3–4cm wide. If the kale looks a bit tired, refresh in a bowl of cold water for 5–10 minutes, then shake dry.

Meanwhile, toast the nuts and seeds in a dry frying pan over a medium heat for a few minutes until fragrant and lightly browned in parts, shaking the pan often. Tip out onto a plate and allow to cool, then lightly chop the nuts and crush the seeds.

Put the kale into a large bowl with the chilli flakes, a good pinch of salt, the raisins and their soaking liquid. Using a pair of salad tongs or wooden spoons, tumble everything together for a few minutes, lightly crushing the kale against the side of the bowl. You can do this with your hands if you prefer, scrunching and mixing, to get the same softening effect.

Toss the squash through the kale, leave to mingle for 10 minutes or so, then pour any excess liquid out of the bowl (you can drink it if you like!). Now add the Ajo blanco dressing and give it a final toss. Check the seasoning and tweak if necessary with salt, pepper and perhaps a touch of lemon juice.

Toast the bread slices, trickle with extra virgin olive oil and place one slice on each serving plate. Pile the salad onto the plates and trickle over the dressing remaining in the bowl to serve.

Swaps and Additions
You can use leafy greens, cavolo nero or Savoy cabbage instead of the kale, and/or ribbons of carrot or parsnip in place of the squash. As ever, play fast and loose with the nuts and seeds too.

Festive Cabbage and Clementine Salad

We like to turn to rich, comforting food in the winter months, especially during the festive season, but that means there's always a role for a crisp, refreshing, zingy salad like this to provide fresh crunch and contrast. Or, you can add lentils or beans to make this a meal in itself (see my suggested swaps and additions, below).

Serves 4

½ medium red cabbage
2 medium carrots, peeled and coarsely grated
75g pitted prunes or dried apricots (unsulphured), roughly chopped
3 tbsp apple cider vinegar (ideally raw)
4 clementines (or easy peelers)
A bunch of parsley, leaves picked and roughly chopped
75g walnuts, broken into pieces or very roughly chopped
Sea salt and black pepper
Extra virgin olive oil to finish

Cut out the stalky core from the cabbage, then use a very sharp knife to shred the cabbage as thinly as possible. Tip into a large bowl and add the grated carrots, prunes or dried apricots and the cider vinegar. You can grate or finely chop the stalky core and add that too.

Halve one of the clementines and squeeze the juice over the salad. Add a pinch of salt and a twist of pepper. Toss everything together well and leave to stand for 15–20 minutes, so the cabbage and carrots soften a little in the dressing.

Add three-quarters of the parsley to the salad and toss well then tip onto a large serving platter and spread out.

Peel the remaining 3 clementines and use a very sharp knife to slice them across into 1cm thick rounds (don't worry if some of the rounds fall apart). Lay the fruit over the cabbage salad. Scatter over the walnuts.

Finish with a trickle of extra virgin olive oil, the rest of the parsley and an extra twist of pepper.

Swaps and Additions
You can swap white cabbage in for the red. And small, firm parsnips or a wedge of celeriac work well in place of the carrots.
Hazelnuts, almonds and pumpkin seeds are all good swaps for walnuts.
To make the salad more substantial, toss 250g cooked Puy lentils or a 400g tin of Puy or green lentils (drained and rinsed), or any tinned beans you fancy, with the carrot and fruit.

Fish Fivers

Fish is, without a doubt, one of the healthiest and most delicious sources of protein we can eat. Oily fish, in particular, is a rich source of readily bio-available omega-3 fatty acids (though even non-oily fish has some), which are really important for protecting our hearts. I love the stuff – oily or otherwise – cooked in any number of different ways. And there is no question in my mind that fish – and shellfish – are to be enjoyed at their absolute best when accompanied by some judiciously selected plants. And I don't just mean the chipped potato!

There's no denying that fish can be expensive. And such a precious food probably should be. However, it packs a huge punch in terms of flavour and goodness, so you don't need a large amount of it in order for a dish to really make a splash, as it were. And being generous with those plant companions, in both quantity and number, is rarely a mistake. That's why I'm proposing at least five of them in all of the recipes in this chapter.

That doesn't make them complicated, by the way. At least, no more complicated than slicing a few veg, plucking a few herbs and sprinkling a few spices (fish *loves* herbs and spices). In truth, my ways of enjoying fish have settled into some dearly beloved favourites down the years, and what follows are the very best and simplest of them. The techniques are tried and trusted, and

the changes I'm ringing are mainly in the plants department, to bring you the widest range of flavours and textures – and, of course, goodness.

Mussels (on page 112) are steamed open and added to a gorgeously veg-packed broth, dominated by fennel and leeks, aromatised by herbs, and enriched with a little cream (dairy or coconut, take your pick). Mackerel fillets (on page 124) are baked on a colourful medley of veg, and sardines (on page 120) are served over a riotous salad of tangy tomatoes, fennel and herbs. And my long-time favourite kedgeree is revisited (on page 127) using barley in place of white rice, cooked into a smoky, creamy, nubbly delight along with leek, onion, celery, spinach and peas – pure comfort in a bowl.

If you're a little nervous about cooking fish, perhaps because of its perceived time-sensitive nature, then I hope you'll be pleased to find some of these recipes particularly straightforward. The fish cakes (on page 122), fish sandwich (on page 131) and fish parcels (on page 128), may be as familiar as they are forgiving. All get another outing here with, I'm immodestly going to claim, a delightfully original crop of plants alongside: a seedy crust and rooty filling for the fish cakes; a satay-inspired spicy nutty spread for the sandwich; and half a garden's worth of ribboned veg and aromatics in the parcels.

When you're shopping for these recipes, I'd love you to choose sustainably caught wild fish, or organic farmed fish, if you possibly can. It's a constantly shifting and sometimes complex subject area, but one way to whittle down the doubt is to consult the Marine Conservation Society Good Fish Guide (they now have an app as well as a website), or to look for fish with the blue MSC tick logo on the pack, designated by the Marine Stewardship Council. All of these recipes are adaptable to multiple fish species, and I've suggested plenty of options to help you select the best fish on the day.

Mussels with Leeks, Fennel and Beans

Smoked Mackerel, Parsley and Potato Salad

Smoked Fish in-the-garden Tart

Grilled Sardines with Tomato and Fennel Salad

Rooty Fish Cakes with Seeded Crumb Crust

Roast Ratatouille Mackerel Fillets

Barley Kedgerotto

Spicy Fish Fillet Parcels

Hot Fish Sandwich with Satay Nut Butter

Mussels with Leeks, Fennel and Beans

*Mussels are among the most sustainable seafoods. They are also quick and easy
to cook and lend themselves to being combined with a lot of veg and herbs.
To make a meal of them – and give a pleasing contrasting texture – fat creamy
beans, like borlotti or butter beans, are a lovely addition. Frozen edamame, or
even peas, also work really well.*

**Serves 4 as a starter
or 2 as a main**

1kg live mussels
1 tbsp oil or a knob of butter
1 large onion, finely sliced
2 medium leeks, trimmed and
  finely sliced
1 large or 2 medium fennel
  bulbs, trimmed and finely diced
3 celery sticks, finely sliced on
  an angle
100ml dry white wine or dry
  cider
3 garlic cloves, thinly sliced or
  grated
200ml hot vegetable or fish
  stock
400g tin borlotti or butter beans,
  drained and rinsed, or 250g
  frozen edamame beans or peas
1 tsp English mustard
2 tbsp crème fraîche or cream
A small bunch of parsley, leaves
  picked and roughly chopped
Black pepper

Put the mussels into a colander and give them a good rinse under
cold running water, shaking them about a bit. If the shells have a
'beard' (clump of wiry threads), pull it off. Discard any mussels with
broken shells, and any that are open and do not close when given
a sharp tap (as these may be dead).

Heat a large saucepan over a medium heat. Add the oil or butter,
then the onion, leeks, fennel, celery and a few twists of pepper.
Turn the heat down, cover the pan and let the veg sweat for about
5 minutes until starting to soften, then take off the heat; set aside.

Pour the wine or cider into a second large pan (one with a tight-
fitting lid) and bring to the boil over a high heat. Add the mussels
with the garlic, put the lid on and cook for 2–3 minutes, shaking
the pan once or twice. Lift the lid. Almost all of the mussels should
be open; if not, stir well, cover the pan and give them another
minute over the heat.

Tip the mussels into a sieve over a bowl to catch the juices;
discard any that are still closed. When the mussels are cool
enough to handle, prise about two-thirds of them from their shells.
Set all the mussels aside.

Add the hot stock to the veg pan, along with the tinned beans,
edamame or peas. Return to the heat and bring to a low simmer.
Cook gently for 5 minutes until the veg are tender.

Tip the shelled mussels into the pan. Carefully pour in the juices
from the bowl too, except for the last bit, which may be a bit gritty.
Stir in the mustard, crème fraîche or cream and three-quarters of
the parsley then add the mussels in shells. Remove from the heat
and taste the broth, adding more pepper if needed. Ladle into
warmed bowls and sprinkle with the remaining parsley to serve.

Curried Version
When sweating the veg at the beginning, add a grated 3cm piece of
fresh ginger and 1 tbsp curry powder or paste. Instead of the stock,
add 200ml coconut milk. Leave out the crème fraîche/cream at the end.

Smoked Mackerel, Parsley and Potato Salad

A little smoked mackerel goes quite a long way, and here it adds its tempting smoky flavour and richness to warm waxy potatoes, green beans and lots of herbs. The green element is almost like a deconstructed salsa verde and mingles beautifully with the warm potatoes and fish.

Serves 4

4 medium smoked mackerel fillets (about 250g in total)
A large bunch of parsley, leaves picked and roughly chopped
A small bunch of basil (optional), leaves picked and torn
A small bunch of spring onions or chives, trimmed and finely chopped
1 tbsp capers, roughly chopped
Finely grated zest and juice of ½ lemon
2 tbsp extra virgin olive or rapeseed oil
2–3 tsp wholegrain mustard
500g new potatoes or salad potatoes (unpeeled)
200g green (French) beans, trimmed
Sea salt and black pepper

Take the smoked mackerel fillets from the fridge about 20 minutes ahead so they are not fridge-cold.

Put all the chopped herbs, spring onions if using, and capers into a large bowl with the lemon zest and juice, extra virgin oil, mustard and some seasoning and mix well to make a dressing.

Peel away the skin from the mackerel fillets and roughly flake the flesh, dropping it into the bowl. Toss to combine with the dressing and set aside to allow the flavours to mingle.

Cut the potatoes into large bite-sized pieces, place them in a saucepan and pour on enough water to cover. Bring to a simmer and cook for about 7–8 minutes, until almost tender. Drop in the green beans and cook for a further 3–4 minutes, until they are tender. Drain the veg in a colander and leave for just a couple of minutes to steam-dry.

While the potatoes and beans are still quite hot, add them to the dressed fish and toss to combine. The herbs will wilt a little with the heat of the veg. Leave to sit for 5 minutes to allow the flavours to mingle, then toss again and serve.

Swaps
Replace the green beans with another tender green vegetable, such as asparagus, mangetout or broccoli.
A couple of tins of mackerel or sardine fillets, drained and broken up, can be swapped for the smoked fish, and you can use the oil from the tin instead of extra virgin oil.

Smoked Fish in-the-garden Tart

I love making veg-packed tarts. And I particularly enjoy including smoked fish, usually haddock but sometimes kippers, for the way it contrasts beautifully with the creamy custard, and whatever veg I fold into it too. Choose MSC-certified smoked haddock or kippers if you possibly can.

This version is my favourite so far, featuring courgettes and spring onions, spinach or kale and beans or peas. But the smoked fish is by no means lost in this glorious garden of veg. It's a very relaxed recipe and there are plenty of veg options suggested overleaf.

Serves 6–8

1 quantity Hob-nobby shortcrust pastry, unsweetened (page 250)

A little oil or butter for frying

10 spring onions, trimmed and cut into shorter lengths if long

2 medium courgettes, sliced into 5mm rounds

100g spinach or kale, coarse stalks removed

75g frozen edamame beans or peas (or a mix)

3 medium eggs

150ml double cream or crème fraîche

150ml whole milk

1 tsp English mustard

Freshly grated nutmeg

A small bunch of parsley, leaves picked and finely chopped (optional)

300g undyed smoked haddock fillet (or 200g kipper fillets), skinned and cut into 2cm chunks

50g mature Cheddar or 25g Parmesan, grated

Sea salt and black pepper

Preheat the oven to 180°C/160°C Fan/Gas 4. Have ready a 24cm loose-based tart tin.

Roll out the pastry on a floured surface to a round, large enough to line your tart tin with a bit to spare, turning it over occasionally and dusting with a little more flour as you go. Use it to line the tart tin, pressing the pastry into the corners and trimming away the excess overhanging the rim of the tin.

Place the tart tin on a baking tray. Prick the pastry in a few places with a fork. Line the pastry with baking paper, then add a layer of baking beans or dried beans or rice. Bake for 15 minutes, then remove the paper and beans and return the pastry case to the oven for 5–10 minutes until it looks dry and cooked and is just starting to colour in places. Leave the pastry case to cool a little.

When you are ready to assemble and bake the tart, heat the oven to 170°C/150°C Fan/Gas 3.

Heat a little oil or butter in a medium-large frying pan over a medium heat. Toss in the spring onions and courgettes, and season with a pinch of salt and a generous twist of pepper. Fry gently, stirring often, for about 10 minutes until the spring onions wilt and become tender, and the courgettes soften and lose some of their moisture. (It's okay to let both veg colour a little, but don't allow them to burn.)

Half-fill a medium saucepan with water and bring to the boil. Drop in the spinach or kale, pushing it down so it is covered with water and wilts immediately. After a minute, remove with a slotted spoon and refresh in cold water. Drain and squeeze out as much water as possible, then chop roughly and put to one side.

Drop the frozen edamame and/or peas into the pan of hot water too, then immediately drain and set aside.

Continued overleaf

To make the savoury custard, in a bowl, beat the eggs, cream or crème fraîche, milk and mustard together with a few gratings of nutmeg, a pinch of salt and several twists of pepper. Stir in the chopped parsley, if using.

Arrange the smoked fish chunks evenly in the tart case, checking for any pin-bones as you do so. Arrange most of the veg on and around the fish, holding back a little of each one. Scatter half of the cheese evenly over the surface.

Now carefully pour the custard over the filling to three-quarters fill the pastry case, rather than fill it to the brim. Arrange the remaining veg over the top in a pleasing way, gently prodding the veg into the custard. Scatter over the last of the grated cheese.

Carefully transfer the tart to the middle shelf of the oven and bake for 30–35 minutes, until golden brown on top. Leave to rest for at least 30 minutes before cutting.

The tart is actually best eaten warm or at room temperature, rather than piping hot. And leftovers straight from the fridge are pretty good too. Serve with simply dressed green leaves, such as lettuce or rocket, according to the season.

Swaps
Instead of the courgettes, you can use blanched asparagus or green beans, or slices of fennel, sweating these with the spring onions. Sweetcorn (frozen is fine) works well in place of the edamame/peas. And you can play around with any of these veg, in varying combinations.

Grilled Sardines with Tomato and Fennel Salad

Fresh sardines are a delicious and sustainable choice (our Cornish sardine fishery is MSC-certified), as well as being rich in omega-3s. Ask your fishmonger to gut and scale the sardines for you. A couple of medium sardines per person makes a nice starter; serve 3 larger fish for a main course. If going for a main, you could serve some wholegrain toast, trickled with extra virgin oil, alongside.

When cooking the fish make sure your grill, frying pan or barbecue is piping hot. This gives you the best chance of getting a delicious crispy skin without it sticking to the pan or grill rack.

Serves 4

8 or 12 sardines, scaled and
  gutted
Vegetable oil for cooking

Tomato and fennel salad
400g cherry tomatoes, quartered,
  or 4–5 medium tomatoes,
  roughly chopped (or a mix)
1 small red onion, very finely
  sliced or chopped
1 small fennel bulb, trimmed and
  finely sliced
1 small garlic clove, grated or
  crushed
A good pinch of salt
A handful of chives, snipped
  (optional)
A small handful of mint leaves,
  fairly finely chopped (optional)
5 tbsp extra virgin olive oil
Finely grated zest of 1 lemon,
  plus the juice of ½ lemon
Sea salt and black pepper

To finish and serve
A handful of parsley leaves
Wholegrain toast (optional)
Extra virgin olive oil (optional)

For the tomato and fennel salad, put all the ingredients into a bowl and toss to mix, seasoning with salt and pepper to taste. Leave to mingle while you cook the sardines.

Heat up a griddle pan or large heavy-based non-stick frying pan, or your barbecue, until very hot. If you are cooking inside and your cooker doesn't have an extractor hood, you might want to open the windows, as even the freshest sardines give off a fishy smell!

Rub a little oil over the sardines, and sprinkle them with salt too. Place the fish in the hot pan or on the barbecue and cook without moving for 3–4 minutes.

Now run a thin spatula under the fish and carefully turn each one over. With luck you'll do this without the skin sticking, but if that happens, don't worry, the fish will still be delicious. Cook the sardines on the other side for just 2–3 minutes, then carefully remove from the pan or barbecue, using the spatula again.

Pile the tomato and fennel salad onto a serving platter and arrange the sardines on top. Scatter over the parsley and serve straight away, with wholegrain toast trickled with extra virgin olive oil on the side if you like.

Rooty Fish Cakes with Seeded Crumb Crust

Who doesn't love a fish cake, with a crisp golden crumb crust and tender filling? Both these elements get a plant boost here, with crunchy seeds in the crumb, and fish-friendly celeriac and plenty of herbs in with the fish and potato. The fish cakes can be fried, but I prefer to bake them. They are delicious with a green salad and a simple tomato salsa, or Leeks, greens and caraway (page 190).

Serves 4

300g floury potatoes, scrubbed and cut into 3cm chunks
200g celeriac, peeled and cut into 3cm chunks
400g skinless white fish fillet, such as hake or coley, or MSC-certified haddock or cod
A small bunch of parsley or dill, leaves picked and finely chopped
A small bunch of chives, finely chopped
1 tbsp capers, roughly chopped
1 tsp English mustard
1 egg
20g butter, softened, or 1 tbsp rapeseed oil
A little flour to dust
Oil or fat for brushing
Sea salt and black pepper

Coating

50g fine plain wholemeal flour
1 egg, beaten
1 tbsp milk
100g wholemeal breadcrumbs
2 tbsp sesame seeds
2 tsp chia, flax or poppy seeds (or a mix)

To serve

Tomato salsa (prepare as for the salad on page 120, omitting the fennel and herbs)
Green salad

Put the potatoes and celeriac into a saucepan, pour on enough water to cover and add a good pinch of salt. Bring to the boil, lower the heat and simmer for 12–15 minutes until tender. Drain in a colander and leave to steam-dry and cool for at least 15 minutes.

Meanwhile, cut the fish into chunks and place in a food processor with the parsley or dill, chives, capers, mustard, egg, butter or oil, a pinch of salt and a few twists of pepper. Pulse a few times to chop up the fish and combine thoroughly with the other ingredients, but don't blitz to a paste – you want to retain some texture in the fish.

Tip the cooled potatoes and celeriac into a large bowl and mash roughly, keeping some texture. Add the fish and herb mix, and stir to combine thoroughly with the mashed roots.

Tip the mixture out onto a large board, press together and divide into 8 even pieces. Lightly flour your hands and shape each piece into a ball then flatten to a round cake, about 2–3cm thick.

To crumb coat your fish cakes, you will need 3 deep plates or shallow bowls: add the flour to one, seasoning with a pinch each of salt and pepper; beat the egg with the milk in another; and tip the breadcrumbs and all the seeds into the third, mixing well.

Dip each fish cake first into the flour, turning it to coat both sides and the edges, then carefully into the beaten egg, making sure it coats all surfaces, and allowing any excess to drip off. Finally dip into the breadcrumbs and pat gently so they adhere, turning to coat both sides and the edges. Place the fish cakes on a board as you go. Chill for at least 30 minutes to firm up before cooking. (You can keep them in the fridge for up to 24 hours or freeze them.)

Preheat the oven to 210°C/190°C Fan/Gas 6–7. Lightly grease a baking tray with a little oil or fat.

Place the fish cakes on the prepared baking tray and brush all over with a little oil or melted fat. Bake for 10–12 minutes. Take out the tray, flip the fish cakes over and brush them again. Return to the oven for 12 minutes or so, until crispy and golden on both sides.

Serve at once, with a tomato salsa and a green salad (or veg).

Roast Ratatouille Mackerel Fillets

This is a low-stress way of cooking fish. The delicious Mediterranean sauciness of the roast veg complements the fish beautifully, and the fish fillets cook so effortlessly mingled among them. Although I've used mackerel here, this also works brilliantly with fillets of bass, bream, gurnard or red mullet.

Serves 2–4, depending on the size of the fish

2 medium courgettes
1 medium aubergine
2 medium onions
2 medium red peppers, halved, cored and deseeded
1 heaped tsp coriander seeds, crushed
3 tbsp olive oil, plus a little extra for the fish
6 garlic cloves, roughly chopped
250g ripe cherry tomatoes (not too tiny)
8 mackerel fillets
Sea salt and black pepper
Lemon wedges to serve

Preheat the oven to 220°C/200°C Fan/Gas 7.

Cut the courgettes, aubergine and onions into 3cm chunks; cut the peppers into roughly 3cm pieces. Put all the veg into a large roasting tray with the crushed coriander seeds, olive oil, a good pinch of salt and a few twists of pepper.

Toss everything together so it is evenly coated in the oil and seasonings. Roast in the oven for 20 minutes until the veg are starting to blister and soften.

Take the tray from the oven and add the garlic and whole cherry tomatoes. Toss gently to mix with the other veg then return to the oven for another 15 minutes.

Meanwhile, check the fish fillets for pin-bones, removing any you find with tweezers. Lightly oil the fish fillets and season with a little salt and a few twists of pepper.

Lift the roasting tray out of the oven and turn the oven to a grill setting. Lay the seasoned mackerel fillets, skin side up, on top of the veg. Place the tray under the grill for 4–6 minutes, depending on the heat of your grill, until the mackerel skin is bubbling and golden and the fish is just cooked through.

Place 2 fish fillets on each warmed plate with the roast ratatouille veg spooned generously alongside. Add a lemon wedge to each plate, to squeeze over the fish and veg – it cuts the richness of both beautifully. Serve at once.

Barley Kedgerotto

This lovely creamy dish of smoked fish, grains and greens sits somewhere between a kedgeree and a risotto – hence the name. It's a luxurious way to enjoy the flavours of smoked fish and the goodness of whole grains, along with silky greens and popping peas or beans.

Serves 4

200g pearl barley (or spelt)
500g undyed smoked haddock
  or 400g kipper fillets
2 bay leaves
300ml milk (dairy or nut/oat milk)
Oil or fat for cooking
1 large onion, finely sliced
1 leek, trimmed and finely sliced
2 celery sticks, finely sliced
3 garlic cloves, finely sliced
4 medium eggs
150g frozen peas or edamame
  beans, defrosted
100g spinach, coarse stalks
  removed, shredded
A knob of butter
A small bunch of parsley, leaves
  picked and roughly chopped
A small bunch of chives, snipped
  (optional)
Sea salt and black pepper
Lemon wedges to serve

Put the barley (or spelt) into a bowl, pour on cold water to cover and leave to soak for 1–2 hours.

Cut the fish fillet into 2 or 3 pieces and lay in a medium saucepan. Add the bay leaves, then pour on the milk and 400ml water, to just cover the fish. Place over a medium heat and bring the liquid just to the boil. Immediately take off the heat, put the lid on the pan and leave the fish to cook in the residual heat for 5 minutes.

Lift the fish out of the pan with a slotted spoon or spatula and place on a plate; set aside to cool. Strain the cooking liquor into a measuring jug: if there's less than 650ml, top it up with water.

Heat a little oil or fat in a fairly large saucepan over a medium heat. Add the onion, leek and celery with a pinch of salt and get everything sizzling, then lower the heat. Let the veg sweat gently for 5 minutes or so, stirring occasionally, until softened and starting to colour a little. Add the garlic and cook for another 2–3 minutes.

Give the soaked barley (or spelt) a final rinse, then add to the veg in the pan. Stir to ensure the grains are well coated with the oil. Pour on about 300ml of the reserved fish cooking liquor and bring to a gentle simmer. Cook as you would a risotto, letting it bubble gently, stirring often and, as the liquor is absorbed, adding more to keep it wet and creamy. You may need a little more than you have; if so, add a dash of hot water from the kettle. After 30–35 minutes, taste the barley (or spelt); it should be almost tender. If it's still firm in the middle, give it a splash more water and another 5 minutes.

Meanwhile, cook the eggs: bring a small pan of water to the boil, lower in the eggs and simmer for 7–8 minutes, then remove, refresh briefly in cold water and tap the shells to crack them.

When the grain is just tender, stir in the peas or edamame and spinach and cook for 3 minutes. Flake the fish, removing any skin and pin-bones as you do so, and add to the pan, with the butter and three-quarters of the parsley and chives if using. Let rest for a couple of minutes, while you peel and halve the warm eggs.

Place the egg halves on top of the kedgerotto and sprinkle with the remaining herbs. Serve at once, with lemon wedges on the side.

Spicy Fish Fillet Parcels

Opening a paper parcel of fish, veg and spices, so all the gorgeous aromas whoosh up your nose, is always a great treat. There are lots of fun ways to vary the veg and spices here, but this Asian-inspired version is hard to beat.

Ideally, choose 2 large, thick fish fillets (around 300g each) and cut each one into 2 squarish chunky portions. If your fillets are smaller then you'll need to buy 4, one for each parcel.

Serves 4

4 skinless white fish fillets, ideally
 chunky (about 150g each),
 such as hake or coley, or
 MSC-certified haddock or cod
2 small courgettes or
 ½ cucumber
1 large carrot, scrubbed or
 peeled
1 small fennel bulb, trimmed
12 spring onions, trimmed
2 garlic cloves, finely sliced
3–4cm piece of fresh ginger,
 finely sliced
1 large red chilli (not too hot),
 deseeded and finely sliced
4 bay leaves (optional)
2 tbsp toasted sesame oil,
 plus extra to oil the paper
2 tbsp soy sauce
Finely grated zest and juice
 of 2 limes or 1 lemon
Steamed or boiled brown rice
 to serve

Preheat the oven to 200°C/Fan 180°C/Gas 6 and have ready a large baking tray with a rim (to contain any juices). Tear off 4 large sheets of baking paper, large enough to enclose the fish and veg.

Cut the courgettes or cucumber lengthways into fine ribbons, ideally using a vegetable peeler, stopping when you get to the seedy core. Do the same with the carrot and fennel. Slice the spring onions lengthways into thin strips.

Put all of these veg into a large bowl and add the garlic, ginger, chilli, bay leaves if using, sesame oil, soy sauce and the citrus zest and juice. Toss well.

Lightly oil a patch in the middle of each paper square with sesame oil. Pile half of the veg onto the oiled patches, dividing them equally. Place a fish fillet portion on each pile and top with the remaining veg. Gather up the edges of the paper and bring them up around the veg and fish to form an open parcel. Pour the oily, soy juices from the bowl evenly over the veg and fish.

Scrunch the edges of the paper together over the fish and veg to seal the parcels and tie loosely with string. Carefully lift the parcels onto the baking tray. Bake in the oven for 15–20 minutes or until the fish is cooked and the veg are just tender (open one of the parcels to check).

Transfer the parcels to warmed plates and bring to the table for guests to open themselves. Have a bowl of brown rice on the table too, so each person can spoon some into their parcel alongside the fish and veg, to soak up the delicious juices.

Swaps
You can experiment with all kinds of veg and herbs here. Switching from Asian flavours to onions, courgettes, bay leaf, parsley, white wine and butter is a good way to go. A handful of samphire is a nice addition, too. Always slice the veg finely so it cooks quickly alongside the fish.

Hot Fish Sandwich with Satay Nut Butter

You may already know how much I enjoy a hot fish sandwich. This latest incarnation is combined with a delicious satay nut butter, and I like to add a contrasting layer of crunchy kimchi slaw, too. This sandwich works well with white fish fillets, such as haddock or coley, but it's also great with meatier fish like mackerel or bream.

Serves 2

2 skinless fish fillets (100–120g each), such as hake or coley, or MSC-certified haddock or cod
A little light plain wholemeal flour
Oil or fat for cooking
2 bay leaves
2 garlic cloves, crushed
Sea salt and black pepper

Satay nut butter
2 tbsp crunchy peanut butter
½ small garlic clove, crushed or very finely grated
Finely grated zest and juice of 1 lime or ½ lemon
1 tbsp soy sauce

To assemble
2 large, soft wholemeal baps, split
4 lettuce leaves
1 ripe tomato, sliced
2–3 tbsp Kimchi slaw (page 182, optional)

First make the satay nut butter. Combine all the ingredients in a small bowl and mix well, seasoning with a few twists of pepper. If the nut butter seems too thick to spread, stir in a dash of water to loosen it.

Check the fish fillets for pin-bones, removing any you find with tweezers. Season the fish well on both sides with salt and pepper. Dust the fillets with a little flour.

Heat a little oil or fat in a non-stick frying pan over a medium heat. Add the bay leaves and fry until they start to colour (you are using them to flavour the oil and fish so it's okay if they brown a bit).

Add the fish fillets to the pan, along with the garlic, and fry for 3–4 minutes, basting with the oil, until nearly cooked through. Carefully flip the fish fillets over and cook for a minute or so on the other side.

In the meantime, spread the bap bases with a generous spoonful of the satay nut butter. Lay two overlapping lettuce leaves on top, then a couple of tomato slices.

Using a thin spatula or fish slice, lift the hot fish fillets out of the pan straight onto the tomato slices. Top with a spoonful of kimchi slaw if you like.

Sandwich together with the bap tops and squeeze gently to bring the layers together. Eat straight away.

Meat and Many Veg Mains

In the next few pages I'll show you how plants can be the celebrated co-stars and feted cameos of your meat dishes, instead of playing the mere extras to limelight-hogging animal proteins. Gone (with the wind?) are the days of 'meat and two veg'; instead, meat and five, six or seven veg are winning much deserved plaudits…

I've focused on some of the country's best-loved dishes here. A simmering sausage casserole, a piping hot, crisp-topped cottage pie and a gloriously golden roast chicken remain among my favourite things to eat. But I do things a little differently, now I'm living in 30-plants-a-week world: my tastes and my mindset have changed and I'm reaping the rewards of a number of foods.

So, now I mix roots and lentils into my cottage pie filling, and add capers, mustard and parsley to a multi-root mash topping (on page 152), massively bumping up the plant content as well as the flavour. Similarly, the roast chicken recipe (on page 134) includes a healthy helping of brown rice mixed with the cooking juices, roasted fennel and onions, plus bashed nuts and tangy herbs, lemon and sun-dried tomatoes.

This is not about covertly sneaking a few more vegetables into a meat dish 'to hide them from the kids'. It's about rethinking the whole thing so that plants come proudly to the fore. That doesn't mean you have to change the basic structure of the dish, but do shift the proportions plant-wards,

adding all sorts of herbs, spices, veg and even fruit, and correspondingly reducing, relatively, the amount of meat. Not drowning it out by any means, just keeping it pleasingly in proportion.

If you're barbecuing in the summer, rather than grilling a steak on its own, why not put a couple of bunches of spring onions on the barbie too, to char and soften and gain some deliciously smoky notes, then chop and stir them into a herby salsa verde to serve alongside (see page 151). This is a perfect example of how to maximise flavour and opportunity, and get the best out of plants by putting them uppermost in your thinking.

You'll also find a slow-roast shoulder of lamb with a panoply of spices, herbs and garlic, not to mention root veg and pulses (see page 140). Unless you're feeding a crowd, it will give you leftovers for days. And there are some delicious lamb and cabbage leaf parcels (on page 146), boosted with barley and tomato and served with a kraut slaw made thriftily from the cabbage trim.

A vital factor when putting dishes like this together is being more selective with the meat you're eating. I believe this is something we should all be doing anyway. Eating less meat of better quality, is good for us, good for the animals that provide the meat, and better for the planet too. A higher-welfare chicken or shoulder of lamb will indeed cost you more, but with these recipes to hand, you'll be making it go further.

I hope you see this as a chance to choose organic, free-range, grass-fed or, at the very minimum, RSPCA-assured meat. I can promise you that it will not only taste better, but the animals will have led better and healthier lives. And surely that more than doubles the feel-good factor of the 30-plants-a-week approach.

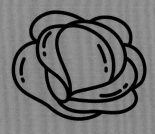

Roast Chicken and Veg with Herby Brown Rice

Rustic on-the-bone Chicken Korma

Sausage and Lentils with Apple and Sage

Slow-roast Merguez-spiced Shoulder of Lamb

Courgette Meatballs in Barley Broth

Lamb and Barley Cabbage Parcels

Steak, Charred Lettuce and Spring Onion Salsa

Cottage Garden Pie

Beef and Squash Tagine

Roast Chicken and Veg with Herby Brown Rice

This is a great way to serve up a roast chicken, with the veg and rice cooked around and underneath it, all picking up the lovely flavours of the bird as it browns in the oven. It's important to pre-soak the brown rice so that it cooks until completely tender.

Serves 6

1 large free-range chicken
  (about 1.8kg)
300g brown rice
1 large or 2 medium fennel bulbs,
  trimmed
4 celery sticks
2 onions, thickly sliced
4 garlic cloves, thinly sliced
2 tbsp olive or rapeseed oil, plus
  a little extra to rub on the chicken
A few bay leaves
A few sprigs of thyme (optional)
About 700ml hot chicken or
  vegetable stock
Sea salt and black pepper

To finish

50g flaked almonds or bashed
  hazelnuts
A bunch of parsley, leaves picked
  and quite finely chopped
A small bunch of mint or tarragon,
  leaves picked and quite finely
  chopped
30g sun-dried tomatoes, roughly
  chopped (optional)
Finely grated zest of 1 lemon and
  juice of ½–1 lemon
30g rocket leaves

Take the chicken out of the fridge 30–45 minutes before cooking to bring it to room temperature. At the same time, rinse the rice, tip into a bowl, cover with plenty of cold water and leave to soak.

Preheat the oven to 220°C/200°C Fan/Gas 7. Cut the fennel and celery into 5mm thick slices on the diagonal. Place in a fairly deep ovenproof dish or roasting tray (that will also fit the chicken with just a little room around it). Add the onions and garlic, trickle over the oil and season with salt and pepper. Toss the veg well then spread out evenly. Tuck in the bay leaves, and thyme if using.

Rub a little oil all over the chicken and season well with salt and pepper. Place on top of the veg, in the centre, tilting the chicken onto one side. Roast in the middle of the oven for 15 minutes, until the thigh and breast start to turn golden brown. Take out the dish or tray and tilt the chicken onto the other side, giving the veg a quick stir too. Return to the oven for 15 minutes.

Take out the dish or tray and lower the oven setting to 180°C/160°C Fan/Gas 4. Lift the chicken onto a board. Drain the rice, give it a final rinse and tip into the dish/tray. Stir to mix with the veg. Place the chicken on top and pour enough hot stock around it to just cover the rice and veg, and come up the sides of the bird.

Return to the oven and roast for another 30–40 minutes, until the chicken is golden and cooked through, and the rice is tender. To check that the chicken is cooked, insert a skewer into the thickest part, where the thigh meets the body: the juices should run clear with no trace of pink. Roast for a little longer if necessary.

Meanwhile, toast the nuts in a dry frying pan over a medium-high heat for a few minutes until golden. When the chicken is cooked, lift it out onto a warmed platter and set aside in a warm place to rest. Check if the rice is cooked: if it's still a bit nutty, stir through a splash of hot stock and return to the oven for 5–10 minutes.

When the rice is done, add the toasted nuts, herbs, sun-dried tomatoes if using, lemon zest, juice of ½ lemon and rocket and stir through the rice. Check the seasoning and tweak with salt, pepper and extra lemon juice if necessary. Carve the chicken and serve up on warmed plates, with a big spoonful of the herby rice and veg.

Rustic on-the-bone Chicken Korma

This is a gorgeous, creamy, nutty chicken curry, with a load of lovely spices that make it really sing. I like to make it with a jointed whole chicken, but it also works well with bone-in thighs and drumsticks. If you buy a whole chicken from your butcher, you can ask them to joint it for you, cutting each breast into two equal-sized chunks.

Serves 5–6

1 large free-range chicken
  (about 1.8 kg), jointed (or
  6 thighs and 6 drumsticks)
2 tsp cumin seeds
2 tsp coriander seeds
5 cardamom pods, bashed and
  seeds extracted
Oil or fat for cooking
1 onion, sliced
3cm piece of fresh ginger,
  coarsely grated
3cm piece of fresh turmeric,
  grated, or 1 tsp ground
3 garlic cloves, finely chopped
2 tsp garam masala (or a mild
  curry powder)
1 tsp dried chilli flakes
400g tin peeled plum tomatoes
400g tin coconut milk
50g ground almonds
Sea salt and black pepper

To serve (optional)
A large handful of coriander
  leaves, chopped
Steamed or boiled brown rice
Raita (page 219)

Take the chicken out of the fridge 30–45 minutes before cooking to bring it to room temperature. Preheat the oven to 170°C/150°C Fan/Gas 3.

Toast the cumin, coriander and cardamom seeds in a large heavy-based pan for 3–4 minutes until fragrant and starting to crackle. Tip the seeds out onto a plate and leave to cool for a minute, then grind to a coarse powder using a pestle and mortar. Set aside.

You will need to brown the chicken in 2 or 3 batches. Add a little oil or fat to the pan, still over a medium heat. When the pan is hot, add several chicken pieces, skin side down. Fry, turning occasionally and seasoning with a little salt and pepper as you go, until nicely browned all over. Remove and place in a fairly deep ovenproof dish or roasting tray. Repeat to colour the rest of the chicken pieces. Set aside.

Now add a little more oil or fat to the pan, followed by the onion, ginger, turmeric, garlic, crushed toasted spices, garam masala (or curry powder) and chilli flakes. Sweat gently for 15–20 minutes over a medium-low heat, stirring regularly, until the onions are very soft but not brown.

Add the tinned tomatoes, crushing them with your hands as they go in (and picking out any stalky ends or bits of skin). Turn up the heat and cook for a few minutes, stirring occasionally to reduce and thicken the liquor. Add the coconut milk, ground almonds and some salt and pepper. Give it a good stir and gently bring up to a simmer.

Pour the creamy tomato mixture over the chicken in the roasting dish or tray. Nudge the chicken pieces around to ensure they are all coated in the sauce and then cook in the oven for 20 minutes. Take out the dish or tray and turn the chicken pieces then return to the oven for 10 minutes.

Serve the curry scattered with chopped coriander leaves if you have some to hand, and with brown rice and/or raita on the side if you like.

Sausage and Lentils with Apple and Sage

When there's a chill in the air, there's nothing better than a big steaming pot of sausage and lentils – with lots of lovely veg in there too. Every version of this I make is a little different depending on what's in the garden or the larder. The apple and sage finish is a brilliant addition from Kitty Coles, who helped test many of the recipes in this book.

Serves 6

Oil or fat for cooking
6 well-seasoned butcher's
  sausages
2 tsp fennel or caraway seeds
  (optional)
2 large onions, chopped
2 large or 3 medium carrots,
  scrubbed or peeled and
  roughly chopped
3 celery sticks, chopped
200g celeriac, peeled and cut
  into 2cm chunks
4 garlic cloves, finely sliced
2 tsp sweet smoked paprika
200g Puy, green or brown lentils
2 sprigs of rosemary, leaves
  picked and finely chopped
3 sprigs of thyme
2 tbsp English mustard
1 heaped tbsp tomato purée
800ml vegetable or chicken stock
100g kale or cavolo nero, coarse
  stalks removed, roughly chopped
Sea salt and black pepper

Topping (optional)
1 large or 2 medium eating apples
12–15 sage leaves

Heat a little oil or fat in a large flameproof casserole over a medium heat. Add the sausages and cook for 5–7 minutes, turning, until browned. Remove with a slotted spoon and set aside on a plate.

Toss the fennel or caraway seeds, if using, into the pan and fry for a minute or so, then add the onions, carrots, celery and celeriac. Cook for 10–12 minutes until the veg are starting to soften, stirring often and scraping up any brown bits from the sausages. Add the garlic and cook for another couple of minutes.

Now add the paprika, lentils, rosemary, thyme, mustard and a few twists of pepper. Spoon in the tomato purée and stir well. Cut each sausage into 3 or 4 pieces and add back to the casserole. Pour on the stock, then add enough water just to cover everything. Stir well and bring to a simmer.

Lower the heat and simmer very gently, uncovered, for 25 minutes or so, stirring occasionally, until the veg and lentils are tender. Stir in the kale or cavolo and simmer for a further 5 minutes.

Meanwhile, prepare the apple and sage topping if you fancy it. Quarter and core the apple(s) and cut into 3cm chunks. Heat a little oil or fat in a small frying pan over a medium-high heat, then add the apple(s). Fry for 3 minutes until glazed, tossing and stirring occasionally, and seasoning with a pinch of salt and a twist of pepper halfway through. Tip into a warmed bowl. Add a dash more oil to the pan, toss in the sage leaves and fry for 1–2 minutes to crisp up.

Taste the casserole for seasoning, adding more if needed. Ladle into warmed plates or bowls and top each portion with a spoonful of apples and a few crispy sage leaves, if serving.

Swaps and Additions
Use swede or turnips instead of the celeriac, and/or spinach or chard in place of the kale. For a spicier version, use chorizo sausages: cut into 1cm chunks and fry to release their spicy fat before adding the veg. To vary the topping, try adding a few crumbled chestnuts to the pan with the apple(s).

Slow-roast Merguez-spiced Shoulder of Lamb

Lamb shoulder, when cooked long and slow like this, becomes meltingly tender and richly flavourful. If you can source hogget (a sheep of around 14–18 months that's had a second spring of grazing), even better. The gorgeous spice mix not only flavours the meat, but creates highly seasoned juices during cooking for the plentiful vegetables and beans to soak up.

I've suggested serving the lamb with a simple green salad, but it would also be great with Radicchio and friends (page 102) or Lemony green polenta (page 199).

Serves 6–8

1 shoulder of lamb, on the bone
  (about 2–2.5kg)
1 tsp fennel seeds
1 tsp caraway seeds
2 tsp cumin seeds
1 tsp coriander seeds
1 tsp black peppercorns
1 tsp dried chilli flakes
2 tsp sweet smoked paprika
6 garlic cloves, peeled
6 tbsp vegetable oil
3 onions, cut into chunky wedges
6 sprigs of thyme or rosemary
2 bay leaves
1 head of celery
5 large carrots
½ medium swede or 2 turnips
  (optional)
200ml white wine
2 x 400g tins chickpeas or butter
  beans, drained and rinsed
Finely grated zest and juice of
  ½ lemon
Flaky sea salt and black pepper

To serve

2 lettuces, leaves separated
½ cucumber, thinly sliced
A small bunch of parsley, leaves
  picked
Finely grated zest and juice of
  ½ lemon
3 tbsp extra virgin olive oil

Take the lamb out of the fridge about an hour before cooking to bring it to room temperature.

Preheat the oven to 200°C/180°C Fan/Gas 6.

If you have time, toast the fennel, caraway, cumin and coriander seeds with the peppercorns in a dry frying pan over a medium heat for a minute or so, until fragrant (this boosts the flavour but isn't essential). Tip the mixture out onto a plate and leave to cool for a minute or two.

Using a pestle and mortar, crush the spice seeds and peppercorns to a coarse powder. Add the chilli flakes, paprika, 2 crushed garlic cloves, 2 tsp flaky sea salt and the oil and mix to a paste.

Lightly score the surface of the meat using a sharp knife, making shallow slashes just a few millimetres deep and 1–2cm apart. Rub about two-thirds of the spice paste all over the lamb shoulder, underneath as well as on top, and especially into the cuts.

Lay the lamb shoulder in a large roasting tray (one that has plenty of room for the veg to come) and roast in the oven for 30 minutes.

In the meantime, in a bowl, toss the onion wedges with the rest of the spice mix until evenly coated.

Take the roasting tray from the oven and lift out the lamb shoulder onto a board. Distribute the spiced onion around the tin, scatter over the thyme or rosemary and bay leaves then place the meat back in. Cover the tray with foil and return to the oven.

Lower the oven setting to 140°C/120°C Fan/Gas 1 and cook the lamb shoulder for a further 3 hours or so.

In the meantime, prepare the rest of the vegetables. Separate the celery sticks and cut each in half. Scrub or peel the carrots and cut these in half. Peel the swede or turnips, if using, and cut into chunky wedges.

Continued overleaf

Remove the roasting tray from the oven and lift the meat out onto the board again. Add all the other veg to the tray, with the rest of the garlic cloves. Pour the wine and 200ml hot water over the veg, then replace the meat and return to the oven.

Roast for another 2½–3 hours, taking the tray out once or twice to baste the meat with the spicy juices if you like. The meat is ready when it is so tender you can pretty much pull it off the bone.

Lift the meat onto a large warmed platter and leave to rest in a warm place, covered with the foil, while you turn your attention to the veg and juices in the roasting tray.

If the juices are quite fatty, carefully pour off some of the fat. Add the chickpeas or butter beans to the tender roasted veg, along with the lemon zest and juice, spreading them around the tray and basting with the juices. Place back in the oven for 20 minutes.

Meanwhile, to prepare the salad, toss the lettuce, cucumber, parsley and lemon zest in a bowl with the lemon juice and extra virgin olive oil, seasoning with salt and pepper to taste.

Carve, pull or tear generous strips of lamb off the bone and serve on warmed plates with plenty of the tender veg and rich spicy roasting juices. Bring the salad to the table – I like to have it after, rather than with the lamb.

Swaps and Additions
This is a versatile dish with scope for lots of seasonal veg swaps. Other roots, such as beetroot, parsnips and celeriac, and wedges of squash, can all be swapped for the carrots and swede, or added in as well. Thickly sliced potatoes, ideally a waxy kind, can also be included. Instead of the chickpeas, add 500g frozen peas (defrosting them first). You can also toss a couple of handfuls of greens such as kale or cavolo into the veg with the beans, so they wilt down for the final 20 minutes.

Courgette Meatballs in Barley Broth

When courgettes are in season they come in abundance and I find myself trying to get them into a lot of meals. Here, they work very well grated and added to the meatballs, helping to keep them moist and tender. The meatballs are served in a delicious broth with barley, peas and beans, topped with a dollop of courgette raita.

Serves 4–5

1 medium or 2 small courgettes
  (about 250g)
500g lamb or beef mince
2 garlic cloves, finely grated
A small handful of parsley, leaves
  picked and very finely chopped
1 tbsp dried oregano (optional)
1 tsp fennel or caraway seeds,
  crushed
1 egg, beaten
Oil or fat for cooking
Sea salt and black pepper

Pearl barley broth

2 onions, finely chopped
1 large or 2 medium fennel bulbs,
  trimmed and finely chopped
  (optional)
2 garlic cloves, finely chopped
100ml white wine (optional)
1 litre vegetable or chicken stock
100g pearl barley or quick-cook
  spelt, well rinsed
100g frozen peas
100g frozen broad beans or
  edamame beans (optional)
Juice of ½ lemon, or to taste

To serve

Raita with added courgette
  (page 219)
Parsley and/or mint leaves
Extra virgin olive oil

Coarsely grate the courgette(s) and toss with a good pinch of salt. Place in a colander over the sink for 20 minutes to draw out some of the water. Then squeeze out as much water from the grated courgette as you can with your hands.

In a bowl, combine the grated courgette, mince, garlic, parsley, oregano if using, crushed fennel or caraway seeds, some salt and pepper, and the beaten egg. Mix well and scrunch everything together with your hands until evenly combined.

Divide the mixture into 16 even-sized pieces and shape into balls, rolling them firmly in the palms of your hands. Place on a tray or plate and chill in the fridge for an hour to firm up a bit (if time).

Heat a little oil or fat in a large heavy-based saucepan. When hot, brown the meatballs in batches over a fairly high heat, turning to colour evenly on all sides. Remove and set aside on a plate.

Now prepare the broth. Heat a little more oil or fat in the pan and lower the heat. Add the onions, with the fennel if using, and fry for 10 minutes until softened and light golden, stirring occasionally and loosening any bits of meat from the bottom of the pan. Toss in the garlic and fry for another 2 minutes, then add the wine if using.

Now pour in the stock and bring to a simmer. Add the barley or spelt, with a pinch of salt, and simmer for 25–30 minutes until it is tender but still a little nutty. The grain will thicken the broth a little, but there should be plenty of liquid still in the pot – you can always add a splash more stock or hot water.

Add the meatballs back to the pot and simmer in the broth for 5 minutes. Add the peas, and broad beans or edamame beans if using, return to a simmer and cook for 2–3 minutes. Turn off the heat. Check the seasoning, adding salt, pepper and lemon juice to taste.

Put 3 or 4 meatballs into each warmed serving bowl and ladle in plenty of barley, veg and liquor. Add a dollop of courgette raita, scatter over a few parsley and/or mint leaves and trickle on a little extra virgin olive oil to serve.

Lamb and Barley Cabbage Parcels

These parcels are inspired by Eastern European flavours. I've used the larger outer leaves of the cabbage to wrap the parcels, and the tender inner leaves to make a kraut slaw to serve on the side.

Wrapping the parcels is one of those jobs that takes a little time and care, but serving up the finished dish to friends and family is very satisfying. For convenience, you can prepare the parcels a day ahead, refrigerate them overnight and do the final baking the following day.

Serves 4

1 large (or 2 smaller) Savoy
  cabbage(s)
Oil or fat for cooking
300g lamb mince
1 onion, finely sliced
1 carrot, scrubbed or peeled
  and fairly finely chopped
1 celery stick, thinly sliced
2 garlic cloves, finely sliced
  or grated
½ tsp dried chilli flakes
50g pearl barley (or spelt)
400g tin peeled plum tomatoes
A glass of white wine
400ml vegetable or lamb stock
A bunch of dill, roughly chopped,
  or parsley, leaves picked and
  finely chopped
Sea salt and black pepper

To serve
Kraut slaw (page 182), made
  with the inner cabbage leaves

First prepare the Savoy cabbage(s). Remove and discard any very tough or damaged dark outer green leaves. Then carefully remove 12–14 large, bright green leaves for the parcels. (Use the inner heart for the kraut slaw.)

Place the large cabbage leaves, spine side up, on a large board and use a potato peeler to shave down the stalk (to make the leaves more pliable for wrapping); don't worry if they rip a little.

Immerse the whole cabbage leaves, a few at a time, in a large pan of simmering salted water for 2 minutes then drain and refresh in cold water; drain well and set aside.

To make the filling, place a large, wide ovenproof pan over a medium heat and add a little oil or fat. When hot, add the lamb mince with some salt and pepper and brown for 5–10 minutes, using a wooden spoon to break up the meat as it fries. If the lamb releases a lot of fat, pour this off. Remove the meat from the pan with a slotted spoon and set aside on a plate.

Now add the onion, carrot and celery to the pan and sauté over a medium-low heat for about 10 minutes until softened and lightly coloured. Add the garlic and chilli flakes, stir and cook for another minute or so.

Add the barley (or spelt) and tinned tomatoes, crushing them with your hands as they go in (and picking out any stalky ends or bits of skin). Stir well, increase the heat and cook for 5 minutes, to reduce the liquor until rich and saucy.

Return the browned mince to the pan and pour in the wine and stock. Season with salt and a few twists of pepper, stir well and bring back to a gentle simmer. Cook for 20 minutes or so, until the grain starts to swell and is becoming tender. Remove from the heat and stir through the dill or parsley. Set a colander over a bowl, tip the lamb filling into the colander and let the liquor drip through for 5 minutes. Keep this liquor.

Continued overleaf

Preheat the oven to 200°C/180°C Fan/Gas 6.

To make each parcel, lay a cabbage leaf on a board and place a heaped tablespoonful of the lamb filling in the centre. Fold both ends of the cabbage leaf over and fold the sides over the filling, creating a tightly packed parcel.

Place the parcel back in the pan, with the fold underneath to help secure it. Repeat to make the rest of the parcels. Ideally, they should fit snugly in the pan in a single layer. Pour the strained liquor on top.

Place the pan in the oven and bake the cabbage parcels for 25–30 minutes until they are golden on top.

Serve 2 or 3 cabbage parcels per person with any remaining juices spooned over, with a generous pile of kraut slaw alongside.

Swaps and Additions
Other cabbage varieties with robust leaves, like Hispi or January King, can be used instead of Savoy.
Different root veg, such as celeriac, swede, parsnip or even Jerusalem artichokes, can be swapped for the carrots.
You could also throw a couple of handfuls of defrosted frozen peas into the filling just before you stir through the chopped herbs.
And you can up the spices if you like. Try adding 1 tsp each ground cumin and ground coriander to the softened veg with the garlic and chilli flakes.

Steak, Charred Lettuce and Spring Onion Salsa

It's always worth lighting the barbecue in decent weather to get a nice char on the steak and veg, but this also works well in a pan, as described here. The veg will pick up the flavours of the seared steak, more than they would on the bars of the barbecue. The charred spring onion salsa verde is a lovely recipe in itself and would be great spooned over many things, including Roast chicken and veg with herby brown rice (page 134) or the roast fennel and leeks on page 166, in place of the aïoli.

Serves 2

Oil or fat for cooking
1 large rump or sirloin steak, 3cm thick (about 350g), or 2 smaller ones, at room temperature
12 spring onions, trimmed and cut in half if very long
2 Little Gem lettuces, quartered lengthways
A splash of red wine

To finish the salsa

A small bunch of parsley, leaves picked and roughly chopped
A small bunch of mint or basil (or both), leaves picked and roughly chopped
1 shallot or very small onion, finely chopped
1 garlic clove, finely grated
2 tbsp capers, roughly chopped
1 red or green chilli, deseeded and finely diced (optional)
1 heaped tsp Dijon mustard
1 tbsp red wine vinegar or apple cider vinegar (ideally raw)
4 tbsp extra virgin olive oil
A squeeze of lemon juice, to taste
Sea salt and black pepper

Heat a heavy-based frying pan over a high heat. Grease the pan with a little oil or fat and add the steak. Leave to cook for a minute or so, then flip it over. Lightly season the browned side and cook for another minute. Flip the steak again and season the other side.

Continue cooking in this way, flipping and seasoning every minute or so, allowing in total: 3–4 minutes for rare, 5–6 minutes for medium-rare, 6–8 minutes for medium. Transfer the steak to a warmed plate and leave to rest in a warm place while you cook the veg.

Turn the heat under the pan down to medium. Add the spring onions and cook for 5–6 minutes, turning occasionally, until nicely charred but still green in places. Add a splash of water to the pan for the final minute and let it bubble away – the steam will soften the spring onions a little. Scoop the onions out onto a board.

Add a little more oil or fat to the pan, then add the lettuce wedges, cut side down. Cook for 3–4 minutes until nicely coloured on the underside, then flip onto the other cut surface and cook for another 2–3 minutes to get some good colour on that side too. Transfer to a warmed serving platter with half of the spring onions.

Finally, tip a splash of wine into the pan to deglaze it, stirring and scraping up any bits of meat or veg with a wooden spoon or non-metal spatula. Tip the juices into a small bowl.

To make the salsa, finely chop the rest of the spring onions and add to the pan juices with the herbs, shallot, garlic, capers, chilli if using, mustard, vinegar, extra virgin olive oil and some salt and pepper. Taste to check the seasoning and adjust as necessary.

Cut the rested steak into 2cm thick slices and arrange on a warmed serving platter with the seared veg. Spoon over the charred spring onion salsa and serve at once.

Swaps
You can use lamb leg steaks, or lamb chops in place of the steak, allowing a 150g lamb steak or two bone-in chops per person.

Cottage Garden Pie

A cottage or shepherd's pie has always been a family favourite down the generations. My recipe has evolved to include way more veg than my mum used to put in hers – hence the name. I'm delighted to say this version still meets with everyone's approval.

The meat and lentil sauce is versatile and easily turned into a bolognese (add extra passata and omit the Worcestershire sauce) or into a chilli (add chilli powder to taste to the browned meat and two 400g tins kidney beans towards the end of simmering).

Serves 5–6

Oil or fat for cooking
300g chestnut mushrooms,
  roughly chopped
400g beef mince
2 onions, finely chopped
3 medium carrots, scrubbed
  or peeled and finely chopped
2 celery sticks, finely chopped
2 garlic cloves, chopped
200ml tomato passata
400g tin Puy, brown or green
  lentils, drained and rinsed,
  or 250g pre-cooked lentils
1 tbsp Worcestershire sauce
Sea salt and black pepper

Topping

About 600g potatoes, scrubbed
  and cut into large chunks
300g celeriac, peeled, or
  Jerusalem artichokes, scrubbed,
  cut into large chunks
50g butter
75ml milk
A handful of parsley, leaves
  picked and finely chopped
1 tsp Dijon mustard
2 tbsp capers (optional)

Heat a little oil or fat in a large saucepan or sauté pan over a fairly high heat. Add half of the mushrooms with a pinch of salt and fry 'hard' until they release their juices. Keep frying until the juices evaporate and the mushrooms have taken on a nice golden-brown colour. Tip them into a large bowl. Repeat to cook the rest of the mushrooms, adding a little more oil or fat, then add to the first lot.

Add a little more oil or fat to the pan and then brown the mince well, in two batches. Fry over a fairly high heat, breaking the mince up with a spatula as you go and driving off any moisture. Once browned, add each batch to the bowl with the mushrooms.

Turn the heat down to medium-low. Heat a little more oil or fat in the pan and add the onions, carrots, celery and garlic. Sweat over a medium-low heat, stirring often, for 10 minutes, or until softened.

Return the mushrooms, mince and any juices to the pan. Add the passata with a splash of water and bring to a simmer. Lower the heat and simmer gently for 20–25 minutes until rich and saucy, stirring occasionally and adding a splash more water if needed.

Meanwhile, preheat the oven to 190°C/Fan 170°C/Gas 5, and make the mash. Put the potatoes and celeriac or artichokes into a large pan, cover with water and bring to the boil. Simmer, covered, for about 15 minutes until completely tender.

Stir the lentils and Worcestershire sauce into the mushroom and mince mixture. Taste to check the seasoning, then transfer to an ovenproof dish and spread out evenly.

Drain the potatoes and celeriac or artichokes in a colander; leave to steam-dry for a few minutes. Add the butter and milk to the still-hot pan then tip in the veg. Use a potato masher to crush them to a rough mash. Mix in the parsley, mustard and capers if using.

Spoon the mash evenly over the beef filling, roughly forking it to the edges of the dish. Bake in the oven for 15–20 minutes or until the topping is golden brown and the sauce is bubbling up around the edges. Serve with peas and/or wilted spinach or kale.

Beef and Squash Tagine

The key to this gorgeous tagine is marinating the beef in the blitzed onions, herbs and spices beforehand, so the flavours first penetrate the meat and then percolate back into the sauce during cooking. I like to make this with beef shin, but you can use stewing steak or chuck, which won't take quite as long to cook.

Serves 6

1kg beef shin or stewing steak
3 medium onions
A bunch of coriander, leaves
　picked and chopped
3 garlic cloves, roughly chopped
5cm piece of fresh ginger,
　roughly chopped
5cm piece of fresh turmeric,
　roughly chopped, or 2 tsp
　ground
3 tsp sweet smoked paprika
1 tsp cumin seeds
1 tsp coriander seeds
1 tsp ground cinnamon (optional)
½ tsp dried chilli flakes
3 tbsp extra virgin olive oil
Oil or fat for cooking
600ml chicken or vegetable stock
750g squash, such as butternut,
　acorn or kabocha, deseeded,
　skin removed
2 x 400g tins chickpeas or butter
　beans, drained and rinsed
12 dried prunes, apricots or figs,
　halved
Juice of ½ lemon, or to taste
Sea salt and black pepper

To serve (optional)

Brown rice or wholegrain
　couscous
Leeks, greens and caraway
　(page 190)

Cut the beef into 4cm pieces and place in a large bowl. Roughly chop one of the onions and place in a blender with the coriander, garlic, ginger, turmeric, spices, extra virgin olive oil and a large pinch of salt. Blend until fairly smooth, but retaining a little texture.

Spoon the spice paste over the meat, then thoroughly massage it into the meat, using your hands. Cover the bowl and leave to marinate in the fridge for at least 3 hours, or overnight if time.

Take the bowl from the fridge and transfer the meat to a plate, scraping off the excess marinade back into the bowl as you go. Leave the beef to sit at room temperature for 20–30 minutes; keep the marinade in the bowl.

Preheat the oven to 140°C/120°C Fan/Gas 1.

Cut the remaining peeled onions into 6 wedges each. Heat a little oil or fat in a large flameproof casserole or ovenproof pot over a high heat, then brown the beef in batches until evenly coloured, transferring the pieces to a plate once they are ready.

Turn down the heat a little and add the onion wedges to the pot. Fry for 5–8 minutes until lightly golden on both sides.

Return the beef to the pot, stir through the saved marinade and pour in the stock. Bring to the boil then lower the heat to a very gentle simmer. Put the lid on and cook in the oven for 2 hours for shin, or 1 hour for stewing steak. In the meantime, cut the squash into chunky 5cm pieces.

Remove the lid, stir the squash, chickpeas or butter beans and prunes or other dried fruit into the tagine and top up with a dash of water if needed to cover everything.

Put the back lid on the pot and return the tagine to the oven for 45 minutes–1 hour until the beef is meltingly tender and the squash is cooked but holding its shape.

Give it all a gentle stir, then season with salt and pepper, and add lemon juice to taste. Serve straight away, with brown rice or couscous and greens if you like.

Seven in the Oven

The oven really can work magic on a clutch of great ingredients, bringing them together in a wonderfully melded, harmonious way. Whether you're roasting or baking – or frankly, not too bothered about the distinction – the effect is always more than the sum of its parts. Slide a tray of good things with great potential into the oven, shut the door and leave them to be transformed by the heat, and their proximity to each other. Then you've got a bit of time while your dish is cooking to clear up the kitchen, lay the table and sometimes make a simple dressing to go over, knowing the main task is done and dusted. And when the timer pings and the tray emerges, there are few things more welcoming and impressive to family and friends than a big dish of roasted deliciousness: tempting, golden and smelling wonderful.

You won't find any meat for the recipes in this chapter. There's a bunch of lovely meat dishes in the previous chapter, and quite a few of them get their mojo from the oven. But this one is all about the plants – which absolutely love the oven too! I'll show you how grilling, crisping and caramelising vegetables (and sometimes fruits too) create flavours that are unachievable in any other way. And how the judicious use of nuts and seeds, spices and herbs can finish them to crunchy, aromatic perfection.

The preparation of ingredients to be roasted or baked can also be a real pleasure. I love layering the potatoes and cabbage for the gratin of greens on page 162, placing all the potato slices neatly to form the final layer, and knowing that when it comes out of the oven it will be burnished and crisp and looking glorious. I've made the point before that, when it comes to eating well, a readiness to do a bit of chopping and slicing, crushing or grating will pay you back a hundredfold. But I'm definitely only talking about enthusiasm and curiosity here, not anything that might be pretentiously labelled 'technique'.

It's precisely by lavishing a bit of the same attention on preparation, followed by the fierce surrounding heat of the oven, that we can make plant-based roasts every bit as tempting as roast meat and baked fish. The fennel and leeks on page 166 come from the oven soft and beautifully caramelised, almost like 'pulled veg', and the creamy, tangy preserved lemon aïoli that goes with them make this dish satisfyingly complete. For sheer umami crunch, the crispy crumb on top of my rich, saucy Aubergine cassoulata (page 169), with its bashed nuts and chopped olives, is up there with a proper pork crackling. And my colourful Festive spiced stuffed squash (page 176) will give the finest turkey-with-all-the-trimmings a run for its money!

The recipes that follow deliver plants in spades –
all use at least seven, and there are a few tenners
in there too! But they are not plant-rich just to be
virtuous. They are bold and balanced and bursting
with flavour, so you won't feel you're missing out
on anything.

Roast Summer Veg with Lemony Dressing

Roast Roots, Red Onions and Chimichurri

Layered Gratin of Greens

Roast Brassicas and Butter Beans

Fennel and Leeks with Preserved Lemon Aïoli

Aubergine Cassoulata

Root and Rosemary Hot Pot

Celeriac, Crispy Quinoa and Goat's Cheese

Tomato and Saffron Baked Rice

Festive Spiced Stuffed Squash

Roast Summer Veg with Lemony Dressing

This is a lovely substantial dish, combining grains and spuds with the first early summer greens. The simple lemony dressing sets it off, but it's also great with the Ajo blanco dressing on page 221, or indeed the preserved lemon aïoli on page 166.

Serves 4

100g cracked bulgar wheat, well rinsed

400g new potatoes (skin on)

4 tbsp olive or rapeseed oil

1 tsp sumac (optional)

1 lemon (juice of ½ of it is for the dressing)

12–15 asparagus spears, woody bases trimmed

2 Little Gem lettuces, quartered lengthways

A bunch of spring onions, trimmed

8–10 garlic cloves, bruised

Sea salt and black pepper

Lemony dressing

2 tbsp olive oil

Juice of ½ lemon

To finish

12 mint leaves

Preheat the oven to 220°C/200°C Fan/Gas 7.

Tip the bulgar wheat into a large bowl, add a good pinch of salt and pour on 500ml just-boiled water. Cover with a plate, so that the water cools gradually, and leave to soak for 30 minutes. Drain off any remaining water.

Meanwhile, halve or quarter the potatoes, depending on size, and put them into a large roasting tray (that will take the rest of the veg later without crowding). Trickle over two-thirds of the olive or rapeseed oil and sprinkle with salt, pepper and the sumac if using. Roast in the oven for 25–30 minutes, until the potatoes are golden brown and tender, turning them halfway through.

Drain off any water from the bulgar wheat after its 30 minutes' soaking and fluff up the grains with a fork. Pare the zest from the lemon in fine ribbons, using a vegetable peeler, and set aside, then cut the lemon in half.

Take the roasting tray from the oven and add the bulgar wheat, asparagus, Little Gem, spring onions and garlic. Trickle over the rest of the oil and the juice of ½ lemon, plus the ribbons of zest. Toss everything together well then space out on the tray. Return to the oven and roast for 12–15 minutes until the asparagus is tender and the Little Gem are wilted.

Meanwhile, for the dressing, put the olive oil, lemon juice and some salt and pepper into a screw-topped jar and shake to combine, or whisk together in a small bowl.

Transfer the roast veg to a warmed serving bowl, scatter over the mint and trickle generously with the lemony dressing to serve.

Swaps

Outside of the asparagus season, use florets of broccoli, calabrese or cauliflower, or batons of courgettes and/or a handful of green beans.

Roast Roots, Red Onions and Chimichurri

A super-simple dish that takes on a whole extra dimension once the glistening green chimichurri is trickled on top. I like to keep the carrot skin on, and find the chunkiness of the veg works really well against the chickpeas. Any leftovers would work very well as a packed lunch.

**Serves 4 as a main
or 6 as a side**

2 medium red onions, peeled
4 large or 8 medium carrots,
   scrubbed or peeled
½ medium swede, celeriac
   or large turnip, peeled
4 celery sticks, cut into
   5–6cm lengths
A few bay leaves
2 tbsp oil or melted fat
400g tin chickpeas (regular
   or black), drained and rinsed
100g feta, roughly chopped
   or crumbled (optional)
Sea salt and black pepper

Chimichurri
15g oregano leaves, finely
   chopped (or ½ tsp dried)
1 tbsp apple cider vinegar
   (ideally raw) or wine vinegar
25g parsley leaves, finely
   chopped
1 green chilli, deseeded and
   finely chopped
1 garlic clove, grated or very
   finely chopped
½ tsp salt
3 tbsp extra virgin olive oil

Preheat the oven to 220°C/200°C Fan/Gas 7.

Quarter the onions lengthways into chunky wedges, cut the carrots into chunky lengths and the swede, celeriac or turnip into chunky pieces. Place these veg and the celery in a large roasting tray (or two smaller ones if they don't all fit in an even layer in your largest tin without overcrowding).

Add the bay leaves, season well with salt and pepper and trickle over the oil or fat. Toss to combine and coat the veg in the oil and seasonings. Add a splash of cold water to the tray and place in the oven. Roast for 30–45 minutes, turning the veg once halfway through, until the onions are tender and the roots are caramelised at the edges.

While the veg are roasting, make the chimichurri. If you have fresh oregano, simply put all the ingredients into a small bowl and give everything a good stir. If you are using dried oregano, place in a small bowl with the vinegar and leave to steep for about 5 minutes, then add all the other ingredients and stir well. Set aside.

When the roast veg are almost done, take out the tray and stir through the chickpeas. Return to the oven for 10 minutes to heat them through.

Remove from the oven and transfer the roasted veg to a large, warmed serving plate, or divide between individual plates. If using feta, scatter it over the veg, then spoon over the chimichurri and serve straight away.

Swaps
Use tinned or pre-cooked Puy, green or brown lentils, or any kind of tinned beans instead of the chickpeas.
And, of course, you can swap the red onions with shallots.

Seven in the Oven

Layered Gratin of Greens

This lovely vegan dish was devised by Kitty Coles. It's a delicious layering of creamy greens, cabbage and spuds, topped off with a crispy nutty topping. The topping is lovely but optional, as you can make a delicious and speedier version by simply crisping up the top layer of spuds.

Serves 4

100g cashew nuts
A little olive or rapeseed oil
350ml hot vegetable stock
1 tsp English mustard
2 tbsp vegetable oil or butter
1 large onion, halved and sliced
1 large leek (about 300g),
   trimmed and cut into 5mm
   rounds
3 garlic cloves, finely grated
250g spinach, coarse stalks
   removed, roughly shredded
1 Savoy or January King cabbage
600g floury potatoes, such
   as Desirée or Maris Piper,
   scrubbed
Sea salt and black pepper

Topping (optional)
30g buckwheat groats
30g walnuts or hazelnuts,
   roughly bashed
1 tbsp olive or rapeseed oil
A few sprigs of rosemary, leaves
   picked, or 10 sage leaves,
   chopped

Soak the cashew nuts in cold water to cover for 3 hours. Lightly oil a shallow oven dish (at least 1.5 litre capacity).

Drain the soaked cashews, put them into a blender with the hot stock and mustard and blitz to a smooth, creamy liquid. Season with salt and pepper to taste.

Heat the oil or butter in a large frying pan over a medium-low heat and add the onion and leek with a pinch of salt. Cover the pan and sweat the veg for 5 minutes or so to soften, then remove the lid and cook for a further 15 minutes or until very soft and golden. Add the garlic and cook for 2 minutes, then stir in the spinach and leave it to wilt for 2–4 minutes. Pour in the cashew cream and stir to combine: this creamy mix of alliums and greens is one layer.

Meanwhile, preheat the oven to 190°C/Fan 170°C/Gas 5. Separate the cabbage leaves, keeping them whole. Bring a large pan of water to the boil. Blanch the cabbage leaves in batches, simmering them for just 2 minutes, until pliable but not soft, then drain and refresh in cold water. (Or you can steam them.)

Thinly slice the potatoes into 3mm thick rounds. Arrange an overlapping layer of potatoes in your oven dish, then a thin layer of the creamy cashew greens, followed by an overlapping layer of cabbage leaves. Season with salt and pepper. Repeat these layers then top with a third layer of potatoes. Trickle a little olive or rapeseed oil over the surface then cover with foil and bake for 35–40 minutes.

If you're making the topping, mix the ingredients together in a bowl. Take the dish from the oven and remove the foil. Scatter the topping over the surface, or simply brush the top potato layer with a little more oil. Return to the oven for 10–15 minutes, until the topping, or the top potato layer, is nicely browned and crispy.

Swaps and Additions
Use a Hispi cabbage, kale or cavolo nero instead of Savoy cabbage.
Swap the onion with a couple of shallots and the leek with fennel.
You can also layer the potatoes 50:50 with another root, such as celeriac or parsnips.

Roast Brassicas and Butter Beans

There aren't many veg that don't taste great after a spell in a hot oven, and most of the brassica family lend themselves well. Sprouts and broccoli are great examples and a good combination. And turnips are brassicas too, of course. I like to combine them with shallots or onions, for the irresistible sweetness of caramelised alliums, but also with pear and butter beans. As you can imagine, there are lots of fun variations on this theme (see below). The squeezed-out roasted garlic makes a lovely rich dressing.

Serves 4

3 small turnips, scrubbed and
  quartered
3 banana shallots or small onions,
  quartered lengthways
8–10 garlic cloves (unpeeled)
2 sprigs of rosemary, leaves
  picked
2 tbsp olive oil
200g Brussels sprouts, trimmed
1 head of broccoli, cut into florets
  and halved
1 firm, under-ripe pear, quartered
  and cored
400g tin butter beans, drained
  and rinsed
75g pumpkin seeds
Sea salt and black pepper

Lemon and garlic dressing
8–10 roasted garlic cloves
  (from above)
A small bunch of parsley, leaves
  picked and finely chopped
  (optional)
Finely grated zest and juice of
  ½ lemon, or to taste
3 tbsp extra virgin olive oil
1 tsp Dijon mustard

Preheat the oven to 210°C/190°C Fan/Gas 6–7.

Put the turnips, shallots or onions and garlic into a fairly shallow large roasting tray and add the rosemary and olive oil with a good pinch of salt and a few twists of pepper. Toss well so that the veg are coated in the oil and seasonings then place in the oven and roast for 20 minutes until the shallots are starting to soften and the turnips are turning golden.

Remove the tray from the oven and add the sprouts, broccoli and pear slices. Give it all a good stir then return to the oven for 20 minutes or until everything is golden and the broccoli is a little charred at the edges.

Take out the roasting tray, pick out the garlic cloves and set aside. Add the butter beans, stir through the veg and then scatter over the pumpkin seeds. Return to the oven for 5 minutes while you make the dressing.

To make the dressing, squeeze out the tender roasted garlic flesh from their skins into a screw-topped jar or bowl. Mash with a fork, then add the chopped parsley if using, lemon zest and juice, extra virgin olive oil, mustard and some salt and pepper. Give it a good shake in the jar, or whisk together in the bowl. Taste for seasoning, adding more salt, pepper and/or lemon juice as needed.

Trickle half of the dressing over the roast veg in the tray. Serve straight from the tray, with the rest of the dressing in a bowl on the table for guests to help themselves.

Swaps
Replace the head of broccoli with cauliflower or Romanesco florets. You can swap the turnips with swede, parsnips, carrots, celeriac or Jerusalem artichokes (or a combination of any of these). Scrub the chosen root(s) and cut into 3cm chunks. And/or use an apple instead of a pear. Sunflower seeds, walnuts, almonds and hazelnuts are good alternatives for the pumpkin seeds.

Fennel and Leeks with Preserved Lemon Aïoli

Fennel's mildly liquorice flavour is a delight, especially when the vegetable is cooked in this way: steam-roasted, then uncovered to caramelise the veg, resulting in a rich, buttery, sweet taste.

The vegan preserved lemon aïoli is a lovely accompaniment, created by our River Cottage head chef Connor Reed. It's well worth making a double batch as it's great to dollop on all sorts of veg, both raw and cooked.

**Serves 4 as a main,
or 6 as a side**

2 fennel bulbs, trimmed and
   quartered, saving the fronds
2 leeks or 8 baby leeks, sliced
   in half lengthways
500g small waxy potatoes,
   such as Charlotte, halved
   or quartered if large
75ml extra virgin olive oil
3 garlic cloves, crushed
1 tsp fennel seeds
A few sprigs of thyme or
   rosemary (optional)
A few sprigs of oregano
   (or 1 tbsp dried)
1 preserved lemon, peel only,
   roughly chopped (pulp saved
   for the aïoli)
Juice of ½ lemon

Aïoli

1 large or 2 small preserved
   lemons, plus the de-pipped pulp
   from the above preserved lemon
2 garlic cloves, finely grated
200ml sunflower or other mild
   vegetable oil
50ml extra virgin olive oil
Sea salt and black pepper

First make the aïoli. Cut the preserved lemon(s) into pieces so you can remove any pips but keep everything else. Put the lemon peel and pulp (plus the saved pulp from the other lemon) into a jug blender with the garlic, ½ tsp salt and 75ml water. Pour both oils into a jug.

Blend on maximum power until the mixture is completely smooth then reduce the power to medium and slowly trickle in the oils to emulsify, resulting in a smooth, glossy aïoli. Taste for seasoning, adding more salt and pepper if needed. Transfer the aïoli to a bowl and set aside.

Preheat the oven to 220°C/200°C Fan/Gas 7.

Put the fennel quarters, leeks and potatoes into a large roasting tray or ovenproof dish and add the extra virgin olive oil, garlic, fennel seeds, thyme or rosemary if using, oregano and 100ml water. Season with a generous pinch of salt and a few twists of pepper. Give everything a good toss, cover with a baking tray or foil and place in the oven for 20 minutes.

Take out the tray or dish and remove the lid or foil. Turn the veg and stir through the chopped preserved lemon. Return to the oven, uncovered, for 20–25 minutes until all the veg are tender and golden at the edges. Trickle over the lemon juice and give everything a final toss.

Transfer the vegetables to a warmed serving platter and scatter over the saved fennel fronds. Serve at once, with the bowl of aïoli on the side.

Aubergine Cassoulata

This is a fun splicing of two well-known European dishes, French cassoulet and Italian caponata, which therefore has the potential to offend both nations, but I promise it will delight all who eat it! If you have ready-made tapenade to hand, for the topping you can simply mix the breadcrumbs, nuts and sun-dried tomatoes with 1 tbsp tapenade, omitting the olives, garlic and oil.

Serves 4

2 medium aubergines (about 600g in total), cut into 5cm chunks
4 tbsp extra virgin olive or rapeseed oil, plus extra to finish
1 medium red onion, cut into 8 wedges
3 celery sticks (about 100g in total), cut into 1cm pieces
A few bay leaves
1 tsp sweet smoked paprika
400g tin peeled plum tomatoes
400g tin carlin peas, or cannellini, haricot or aduki beans
A large handful of parsley, leaves picked and roughly chopped
Sea salt and black pepper

Topping

40g walnuts or hazelnuts, roughly chopped
30g black olives, pitted and finely chopped
1 garlic clove, grated or very finely chopped
150g wholegrain breadcrumbs (fairly dry)
2 tbsp olive oil

Preheat the oven to 220°C/200°C Fan/Gas 7.

Put the aubergines into a medium roasting tin or ovenproof dish and season with salt and pepper. Trickle over 3 tbsp extra virgin oil and toss to coat. Roast in the oven for 20–30 minutes, until the aubergines are softened and lightly golden.

Remove from the oven and add the onion, celery, bay leaves and smoked paprika. Trickle over the remaining extra virgin olive oil, toss to mix and return to the oven for 20 minutes.

While the veg are roasting, prepare the topping. Put the nuts, olives and garlic into a medium bowl and toss to mix. Add the breadcrumbs and season with some salt and pepper. Trickle over the olive oil and mix thoroughly. Set aside while you finish the veg.

Take out the roasting dish and add the tinned tomatoes, crushing them with your hands as they go in (and picking out any stalky ends or bits of skin). Now add the carlin peas or beans, along with 4–5 tbsp of their liquid. Stir gently to mix with the roast veg and return to the oven for 20 minutes.

Take the roasting tin or dish out and turn the oven grill element on to medium-high.

Stir the chopped parsley through the roasted veg, then taste and adjust the seasoning if necessary.

Scatter the breadcrumb mix evenly over the surface and place under the grill for 5–10 minutes (depending on the heat of your grill) until the topping is crisp and golden brown. Keep a close eye on it, to make sure the breadcrumbs don't burn!

Allow the cassoulata to stand for 5 minutes or so before serving. A leafy green salad is an ideal accompaniment.

Root and Rosemary Hot Pot

This is a wonderful medley of chunky winter roots, with the addition of wholesome, hearty butter beans to give body and creaminess, all topped off with a crispy potato crust. A lovely vegan version of a meaty hot pot.

Serves 4

3 large carrots, scrubbed or peeled
2 medium parsnips, scrubbed or peeled
2 red onions, quartered
3 sprigs of rosemary
3 bay leaves
A few sprigs of thyme (optional)
½ tsp dried chilli flakes
2 tbsp rapeseed or olive oil
About 300ml vegetable stock
1 tbsp tomato purée
400g tin butter beans, drained and rinsed
Sea salt and black pepper

Potato topping

300g large waxy potatoes (skin on)
2 tbsp vegetable oil or melted fat

Preheat the oven to 200°C/180°C Fan/Gas 6.

Cut the carrots and parsnips into chunky pieces on the diagonal and place in a large roasting tray with the onions. Add the herbs, chilli flakes and some salt and pepper, trickle over the oil and toss it all together. Roast on the top shelf of the oven for 30 minutes.

In the meantime, pour the vegetable stock into a jug and whisk in the tomato purée.

Take the tray from the oven – the veg should be golden and starting to soften, but still a little firm when poked with a knife. Transfer them to a deep 20–23cm baking dish or casserole.

Add the butter beans to the veg and give everything a good stir. Pour on enough stock to just cover everything (you may need a little more or a little less depending on the size of your dish).

Slice the spuds very thinly into 5mm thick slices, rinse and pat dry. Toss with the oil or melted fat and some salt and pepper. Arrange the potato slices overlapping over the vegetables. Cover the dish with foil (or place the lid on the casserole if using) and lower the oven setting to 170°C/150°C Fan/Gas 3. Bake for 30 minutes or until the potatoes are tender.

Take out the dish and remove the foil or lid. Turn the oven setting back up to 200°C/180°C Fan/Gas 6. Return the hot pot to the oven and bake for a further 12–15 minutes until the potato topping is golden and crispy. (You can speed this up if you use an oven grill setting, but keep a close eye on it to make sure the topping doesn't burn!)

Dish the hot pot up onto warmed plates. I like to serve greens on the side, such as my Leeks, greens and caraway (page 190) or a simple green salad.

Celeriac, Crispy Quinoa and Goat's Cheese

The flavour of roasted celeriac compared to raw is a great example of the different pleasures you can get from one vegetable. I love the fresh crunch from the raw, and the deep flavour from the roasted. And, as Tim Spector points out, you also get different nutrients from the same veg when they are cooked, and raw.

The crispy quinoa is an especially delicious part of this dish, so do give it a whirl. Plus, it stays crisp in an airtight container, so any leftovers are on standby for sprinkling on salads, or anytime you want to add a bit of crunch.

Serves 4

200g red or white quinoa
1 medium celeriac, peeled
Finely grated zest and juice of
  1 lemon
4 garlic cloves (unpeeled)
4 tbsp sunflower or rapeseed oil
1 tsp coriander seeds
1 tsp caraway seeds
1 tsp fennel seeds
½ tsp dried chilli flakes
100g green olives, pitted and
  torn in half
A handful of mint, leaves picked
  and roughly chopped
A handful of parsley, leaves
  picked and roughly chopped
150g soft goat's cheese
100g rocket leaves
Extra virgin olive or rapeseed oil
  to trickle
Sea salt and black pepper

Preheat the oven to 200°C/180°C Fan/Gas 6.

Put the quinoa into a saucepan, pour on enough water to cover generously and add a good pinch of salt. Bring to the boil, lower the heat and simmer for 25 minutes until the quinoa grains are swollen and have slightly 'burst'.

In the meantime, using a vegetable peeler, pare a quarter of the celeriac into fine ribbons, or thinly slice it into matchsticks. Place in a bowl with the lemon zest and juice. Season with salt and pepper, toss well and set aside.

Cut the rest of the celeriac into chunky 5cm wedges and tip onto a baking tray. Add the garlic and trickle over 2 tbsp of the oil. Sprinkle with the coriander, caraway and fennel seeds, chilli flakes and a large pinch of salt, then toss the celeriac to coat evenly.

Drain the quinoa when it is ready and spread it out on a tea towel to absorb any moisture.

Tip the quinoa onto a baking tray, trickle over the remaining 2 tbsp oil and season generously with salt and pepper. Toss well and then spread out in an even layer. Roast for 40–50 minutes until the quinoa is crispy and dry, taking out the tray to give it a stir at least every 10 minutes (to ensure the quinoa crisps all the way through).

Roast the tray of celeriac in the oven (below the quinoa) for about 35 minutes, until nicely caramelised on the outside and tender in the middle, stirring halfway through.

Set aside a couple of spoonfuls of the crispy quinoa. Toss the rest with the roasted celeriac, olives, chopped herbs and most of the goat's cheese.

Transfer the roasted mix to a serving platter or individual plates, scatter over the raw celeriac and rocket leaves, dot with goat's cheese, and add a final sprinkle of crispy quinoa. Trickle over a little extra virgin olive oil and sprinkle with salt and pepper to serve.

Tomato and Saffron Baked Rice

This is a brilliant way to cook brown rice with a few other store-cupboard ingredients that really make a meal of it. Do take time to reduce the tomatoes before adding the rice, as this brings a pleasing richness to the final dish.

Serves 4

150g brown rice
2 tbsp oil or fat, plus extra to
  grease the dish
2 medium onions, sliced
3 garlic cloves, sliced
2 bay leaves
400g tin peeled plum tomatoes
400g tin borlotti, pinto or other
  beans, drained and rinsed
A pinch of saffron threads
A few sprigs of rosemary and/or
  thyme
300ml hot vegetable stock
Sea salt and black pepper

To serve
Extra virgin olive or rapeseed oil
  to trickle
A handful of Dukka or Toasted
  tamari seed sprinkle (page 209,
  optional)

Rinse the brown rice and then leave to soak in a bowl of water for 1–2 hours.

Preheat the oven to 220°C/200°C Fan/Gas 7. Lightly oil an ovenproof dish, about 25 x 20cm.

Heat a medium saucepan over a medium heat and add the oil or fat. Toss in the onions with the garlic, bay leaves and some salt and pepper. Allow to sweat gently, stirring occasionally, for 15 minutes until tender.

Add the tinned tomatoes, crushing them with your hands as they go in (and picking out any stalky ends or bits of skin). Simmer for another 10–15 minutes, stirring regularly, until the mixture is rich, bubbling and thick.

Drain the rice and then add to the pan with the beans, saffron and rosemary or thyme. Pour in the hot stock and stir well. Transfer the contents of the pan to the oiled ovenproof dish, cover with foil or a baking tray and cook for 20 minutes.

Take out the dish and give everything a good stir. Return to the oven, uncovered, and bake for a further 15–20 minutes until crusty and golden on top.

Spoon the tomato-baked rice onto warmed plates and finish with a trickle of extra virgin oil. You can also add a generous sprinkle of dukka or toasted seeds, if you have some handy.

This is excellent served as part of a mezze feast, or alongside a dish of Leeks, greens and caraway (page 190) or Creamy, lemony, minty courgettes (page 192).

Festive Spiced Stuffed Squash

I've been stuffing squashes with delicious roast veggies during the festive season, and beyond, for quite a few years now. It's such a brilliant way to bring something crowd-pleasing to the Christmas table that veggies, vegans and omnivores can all enjoy. This is my most plant-rich version yet. My shroomami gravy makes a brilliant saucy accompaniment.

Serves 6–8

1 medium sweet-fleshed squash, about 2kg (a Crown Prince or kabocha-type is ideal)
About 4 tbsp olive or rapeseed oil
8 garlic cloves, peeled and bashed
2 medium red onions, quartered
3–4 celery sticks, cut into 4–5cm lengths
About 350g parsnips or swede, peeled and cut into 2cm chunks
250g Brussels sprouts
2 medium eating apples, cored and each cut into 8 wedges
150g chestnuts (pre-cooked) or walnuts, roughly chopped
Sea salt and black pepper

Spice mix

2 tsp caraway or cumin seeds
2 tsp coriander seeds
2 tsp sweet smoked paprika
1 medium red chilli, deseeded and finely sliced (or a good pinch of dried chilli flakes)
1 tbsp chopped rosemary leaves

To finish and serve

50g Toasted tamari seed sprinkle (page 209, optional)
Shroomami gravy (page 54)

Preheat the oven to 190°C/Fan 170°C/Gas 5. Slice the top quarter or third off the squash and set it aside. Scoop out the seeds from the 'bowl' that is left and then scoop out or trim some of the flesh around the inside of the opening to make it wider. Cut away the peel from the top slice. Cut the flesh from this piece and the trim from the bowl into chunks; set aside.

Brush the inside of the squash with a little oil, season well with salt and pepper and add half of the bashed garlic cloves. Sit the squash on a baking tray and roast for 1–1½ hours, until the flesh is tender. Take out the garlic and set aside.

In the meantime, prepare the spice mix. Toast the seeds in a dry pan over a medium heat for a minute or two until fragrant, tip onto a plate and leave to cool for a couple of minutes, then bash to a coarse powder, using a pestle and mortar. Add the smoked paprika, chilli and chopped rosemary. Season with some salt and pepper and mix well.

Put the reserved squash pieces into a large roasting dish and add the onions, celery, parsnips or swede, roasted garlic and the rest of the fresh garlic. Add 2 tbsp oil and toss the veg in it, then add the spice mix and tumble together, so the veg is well coated with spices. Put into the oven (above the 'whole' squash if that fits) and roast for 20 minutes, until starting to colour.

Take the roasting tray from the oven and add the sprouts, apples and chestnuts or walnuts. Trickle over an extra dash of oil and toss together. Return to the oven for 25–30 minutes or until everything is tender and starting to turn golden.

When the whole squash is tender, transfer it to a warmed large serving platter and heap the rest of the roasted veg, apples and nuts into it, piling the filling high. Any spare veg can be arranged around the squash.

Scatter toasted tamari seeds on top of the filled squash if you like. Serve with the hot mushroom gravy to pass around.

Triple Treat Sides

For all the fun we've been having making plant-laden dishes the centre of attention, I wouldn't want you to think that I take a dim view of putting simply cooked veg 'on the side' of meat and fish. It is an entirely valid way to cook and entertain, and I do it often.

But the way I am increasingly leaning is towards the embellishment of those vegetable sides with a couple (or more) extra plant elements. This is not simply for the sake of racking up the plant count, though it admirably contributes to that end. It's to make them more delicious too. Simply wilted, lightly buttered cabbage is a mighty fine thing to put on the side of a grilled chop, a baked fish, or a shepherd's pie. But wilted cabbage tossed with sautéed leeks and caraway seeds (on page 190) is arguably finer still.

You get my drift. Why keep veg accompaniments solitary, shy and retiring when, with a quick bit of knife work and a sprinkle of something from the store-cupboard you can round them out into something a little more complex and enticing? Bring in some complementary companions, be they another trad veg, or a herb, spice, nut or seed, and you make those classic vegetable sideshows – peas and beans, spinach and kale, carrots and even the humble spud – seriously sing for their supper.

This is what the recipes in this chapter are all about. They are slam-dunk, hands-down winners: super-simple combinations that add extra interest and plant-based goodness to your plate with minimal extra effort. Between them they incorporate a whole medley of veg, fruit and pulses, running the gamut from alliums and apples to squashes and tomatoes, via lentils and even polenta with plenty of seeds and spices and even a little bit of seaweed thrown in. Yet in every case the procedure is simple and time-efficient.

If you are sweating down some courgettes to a rich creamy pulp with garlic and olive oil, why wouldn't you zing them up with fresh mint and the zest and juice of half a lemon too (see page 192)? And if you're putting together a coleslaw, what's to stop you customising the cabbage and carrot with a tummy-loving tumble of kimchi or kraut (see page 182)?

This needn't always be done for the greater glory of a central piece of protein. These dishes work brilliantly as mezze, or sharing plates, as well as side dishes. Have a trio of these triple treats on the table at the same time, and watch the plantometer head for the rafters. They're incredibly versatile like that, and lend themselves well to one of my favourite ways of eating.

A serving of 'Please can you pass me this' with a side of 'I'd love you to scoop me some of that', is just the best soundtrack to a meal. It's a joyous way to bring family and friends together round the table. Though that's not to say that I don't sometimes relish a comforting dish of Sofrito lentils (page 200) or a plate of summery Bashed potatoes, peas and spring onions (page 189) all to myself once in while…

Kimchi (or Kraut) Slaw

Tomato, Red Onion and Bean Salad

Roast Fennel, Apple and Onions

Bashed Potatoes, Peas and Spring Onions

Leeks, Greens and Caraway

Creamy, Lemony, Minty Courgettes

Tomato, Spinach and Onion

Roast Squash with Chilli and Sage

Lemony Green Polenta

Sofrito Lentils

Kimchi (or Kraut) Slaw

You've probably gathered that I love sauerkraut, kimchi and other fermented veg. They are, of course, quite salty and often pungently flavoured, so not everyone loves the intensity of eating them straight up. But they can also be deployed to give a boost of flavour depth and umami notes to other simply prepared fresh veg. Dressing a slaw is one example, bringing fresh and pickled cabbage together. Once you get the idea, you'll come up with all kinds of variations.

This is a great side to put on the table with almost anything, but it's a particularly brilliant way to make a meal of a couple of poached eggs on toast. The yoghurt and mayonnaise are optional, but they do add a lovely creaminess to the dressing.

Serves 4 as a side

½ white cabbage (250–300g)
2 medium carrots, scrubbed or
  peeled
2 tbsp kimchi (or strongly spiced
  kraut, such as my Golden glow
  sauerkraut on page 227)
Finely grated zest and juice of
  ½ lemon (or 1 tbsp juice from
  the kraut)
2 tbsp extra virgin rapeseed oil
1–2 tbsp natural (or plant-based)
  yoghurt (optional)
1 tbsp mayonnaise (optional)
Black pepper

Finely shred the cabbage and tip into a large salad bowl. Grate the carrots and add to the cabbage. Chop the kimchi (or kraut) if it is quite chunky and add to the bowl with the lemon zest and lemon (or kraut) juice. Toss to mix.

Add the rapeseed oil, and the yoghurt and/or mayonnaise if using. Season with a few twists of pepper and toss everything together well. Taste and by all means add some more kimchi (or kraut) if you think it (or you!) can take it.

Ideally, leave to stand for at least 20 minutes to allow the flavours to mingle before serving. You can also keep the slaw in the fridge for up to 48 hours – the fresh cabbage will start to soften and pickle a little bit, which I rather like.

Swaps and Additions
You can certainly use red cabbage instead of white, in which case the Purple-powered kim-kraut on page 228 would be a great way to go.
In place of the carrots, try grated parsnips, kohlrabi or celeriac.
And thinly sliced celery, cucumber or fennel can go in any time you like.

Triple Treat Sides

Tomato, Red Onion and Bean Salad

I love a salad of ripe tomatoes, with a simple dressing of extra virgin oil and salt, leaving the juice of the tomatoes to do the rest. Adding some crushed pulses is a great way to pick up the juices.

Serves 2–4

350g ripe tomatoes, core removed, roughly chopped
½ red onion, or a few spring onions, finely sliced
1 tsp dried chilli flakes
4 tbsp extra virgin olive oil
400g tin cannellini or haricot beans, drained and rinsed
A few gratings of lemon zest (optional) and a squeeze of juice
A small handful of mint leaves
Sea salt and black pepper

Put the tomatoes and onion into a medium bowl and season with salt, pepper and the chilli flakes. Add 3 tbsp extra virgin olive oil and toss together.

Add the beans with a good squeeze of lemon juice, and a few gratings of zest too if you like. Toss together and leave to mingle for 10 minutes or so.

Just before serving, slice the mint into ribbons and add to the salad with the remaining glug of extra virgin olive oil. Toss gently and serve.

Swaps and Additions
You can chop a couple of plums or a peach and add in, to create that pleasing interplay of flavours featured in the Purple panzanella (page 98). In place of white beans, you can use other tinned or pre-cooked pulses, such as Carlin peas, kidney beans or lentils.

Roast Fennel, Apple and Onions

Roasting these three things together is rather magical. The result is sweet and aromatic, yet still somehow richly savoury too. It makes a fab veggie supper served with my Sofrito lentils on page 200. It's also a perfect side for roast chicken or pork. And there are plenty of swaps and additions to play with (see below).

Serves 2–3

2 fennel bulbs, trimmed, each
   cut into 8 wedges
2 medium-large onions, each
   cut into 8 wedges
3 garlic cloves
1 tsp fennel seeds
3 tbsp olive oil
1 crisp, tart eating apple, such
   as Cox, Braeburn or Russet
6–8 sage leaves, roughly
   chopped (optional)
Flaky sea salt and black pepper

Preheat the oven to 220°C/200°C Fan/Gas 7.

Put the fennel and onions into a roasting tray or ovenproof dish and add the whole (peeled) garlic cloves, fennel seeds and olive oil. Season with salt and pepper and give it all a good toss then place in the oven. Roast for 15 minutes, until the veg start to take on some colour.

In the meantime, quarter and core the apple then cut into large chunks. Take the dish from the oven and add the apple chunks, with the sage if using. Toss to combine with the roasted fennel and onion.

Return the dish to the oven for 10–15 minutes until everything is golden and caramelised. Some apple varieties will hold their shapes, but others may collapse – if this happens, just stir everything together.

Taste to check the seasoning and adjust if necessary, then serve hot from the oven.

Swaps and Additions
You can swap or add in any of the following to ring the changes, or simply boost your plant count: a medium leek as well as, or instead of, the onion; a pear as well as, or instead of, the apple; a few celery sticks in addition to, or to replace, the fennel.

Bashed Potatoes, Peas and Spring Onions

Whenever I've had buttery new potatoes and peas on my plate at the same time, I've always loved squishing them together with my fork and eating the combination. So, here's a dish that makes that happen, and tosses in a couple more goodies to boot! This is great to serve as part of a veggie mezze spread, or indeed as an accompaniment to meat or fish.

Serves 3–4

400g small new potatoes, scrubbed but skin on (halved or quartered if larger)
200g fresh or frozen peas
2 tbsp extra virgin olive or rapeseed oil
A knob of butter (optional, leave out for a vegan dish)
A bunch of spring onions, trimmed and chopped
A handful of mint, leaves picked
A handful of parsley, leaves picked
Sea salt and black pepper

Put the potatoes into a saucepan, cover with cold water and add a pinch of salt. Bring to the boil and simmer for 12–15 minutes until just tender.

Add the peas to the pan and cook for another 3 minutes – the spuds will now be tender enough to crush easily. Drain the spuds and peas in a colander.

Return the hot pan to a low heat and add the extra virgin oil, with the butter if using. Toss in the spring onions and sweat gently over a low heat for a few minutes, just to soften them a little.

Return the still-hot potatoes and peas to the pan, and stir to combine with the spring onions and oil/butter.

Now add three-quarters of the mint and parsley to the pan and put the lid on. Holding the lid and pan tightly together with an oven mitt or heavy-duty cloth, shake the pan vigorously to break up the spuds. Alternatively, or as well, you can use the back of a wooden spoon to crush the spuds. You are not trying to mash them, just break a few apart and rough them up so they mingle nicely with the peas, onions, herbs and oil/butter.

Pile the veg into a warmed serving dish, scatter over the remaining herbs and take to the table.

Swaps and Additions
Try adding broad beans (fresh or frozen) instead, or as well as, the peas. And if you want a super-quick and easy version of this dish, instead of the spring onions, mint and parsley, add a couple of generous spoonfuls of Seven-plant pesto – any of the variations on page 216 will go very nicely.

Leeks, Greens and Caraway

Leeks become deliciously sweet and tender when gently sweated for a while, making them the perfect foil for the punchy taste of cabbage. Caraway seeds add a lovely aromatic note here, and a nibblesome texture too.

Serves 4

2 leeks, trimmed and well washed
25g butter or olive oil, plus extra
  to serve
1 tsp caraway seeds
1–2 tsp dried seaweed flakes
  (optional)
2–3 garlic cloves, finely grated
½ medium cabbage, such as
  Savoy, Hispi or January King
Sea salt and black pepper

Thinly slice the leeks into 5mm thick slices, slightly on the diagonal; set aside.

Melt the butter or heat the oil in a large saucepan over a medium-high heat. Add the caraway seeds and allow to sizzle for a minute or so.

Now add the leeks with a pinch of salt, and the seaweed flakes if using. Give it all a good stir and sweat for a few minutes, then turn down the heat to medium.

Put the lid on the pan and sweat for 10–12 minutes, lifting the lid off to stir occasionally. If the leeks start to colour, just add a splash of water then continue. Add the garlic, stir and sweat for another couple of minutes.

In the meantime, shred the cabbage and cook it briefly: either steam it for 5 minutes or simmer in lightly salted water to cover for 3 minutes. Drain and set aside until the leeks are done.

Add the cabbage to the leeks, season well with salt and pepper and cook together for just a couple of minutes. Toss with a knob of butter or a dash of olive oil, add a final twist of pepper, then serve.

Swaps and Additions
You can easily double up the alliums here, adding a sliced onion or a couple of sliced shallots with the leeks. And you can do the same with the greens – use two types of cabbage or add in some kale or spring greens. You can also use cumin or fennel seeds instead of, or as well as, caraway.

Triple Treat Sides

Creamy, Lemony, Minty Courgettes

Courgettes are one of the great summer glut vegetables. Some years I'm picking them two or three times a week from July to September, but I never tire of them because there are so many lovely ways to cook them. This is one of my favourites. Cooking the courgettes slowly, so they give up their water and stew in their own juice with extra virgin oil, makes them wonderfully rich and creamy.

It's a great side, served hot or at room temperature; it will keep in the fridge for a few days, too. It's also very delicious as a bruschetta – served on wholegrain toast that's been lightly rubbed with a garlic clove and trickled with extra virgin oil. And I love to make it with both green and yellow courgettes for the fabulous colour combo.

Serves 2

3–4 courgettes (about 400g
   in total)
2 tbsp extra virgin rapeseed or
   olive oil, plus extra to finish
2 garlic cloves, grated
Finely grated zest and juice of
   ½ lemon
A small sprig of thyme, leaves
   picked (optional)
A small bunch of mint, leaves
   picked
Sea salt and black pepper
Parmesan shavings to finish
   (optional, not for a vegan
   version)

Slice the courgettes into thin discs (the slicing side of a box grater is handy for this).

Heat the extra virgin oil in a fairly large frying pan over a medium heat, adding the courgettes almost straight away. Add the garlic, lemon zest, thyme if using, and a pinch of salt. Sauté for about 5 minutes, turning up the heat a bit as they release some of their liquid. Let it bubble away, stirring occasionally, then turn the heat down once the liquid has almost all evaporated.

As the courgettes become meltingly tender, you can break them up with a wooden spoon. After about 20 minutes you'll have a rough but rich and fragrant pulp. Cook for longer if you like, for another 10–15 minutes even – but do so gently and carefully to ensure they don't catch or even brown.

In the meantime, slice the mint into fine ribbons. When the courgettes are cooked to your liking, take the pan off the heat and stir in the lemon juice and most of the mint. Taste to check the seasoning, adding salt and pepper as needed.

If serving as a side, transfer the courgettes to a warmed serving dish, scatter over the rest of the mint and finish with an extra trickle of your chosen oil, and Parmesan shavings if you like. Alternatively, pile onto wholegrain toast, or toss with wholegrain pasta of your choice, then finish with the remaining mint, a trickle of extra virgin oil and Parmesan, if using.

Spicy Version
To spice up the courgettes, add some finely chopped red chilli, or a pinch of dried chilli flakes, towards the end of cooking.

Tomato, Spinach and Onion

This is a great side to any meat or fish dish, and it can be deployed in many other roles. It's an ideal base for a shakshuka, for example, but also lovely stirred through pasta or simply served up with poached eggs and toast. And I like to scoop out a few ladlefuls into a jar before I add the greens so I've got a handy portion of excellent tomato sauce at the ready.

Serves 4

Oil or fat for cooking
2 onions, finely chopped
3 garlic cloves, finely sliced or
   grated
2 x 400g tins peeled plum
   tomatoes
2 tbsp olive oil
200g spinach or chard, coarse
   stalks removed, roughly
   shredded
2 tbsp capers or green pitted
   olives (optional)
Sea salt and black pepper

Heat a little oil or fat in a medium saucepan over a medium heat. Add the chopped onions, with a good pinch of salt, and sauté for 10–12 minutes until soft and golden. Toss in the garlic and cook for another couple of minutes.

Now add the tinned tomatoes, crushing them with your hands as they go in (and picking out any stalky ends or bits of skin). Simmer gently for 20–30 minutes until the sauce is reduced and thickened.

Add the olive oil, followed by the shredded spinach or chard, stirring this into the sauce to encourage it to wilt. Stir in the capers or olives if using. Cook for a further 5 minutes, stirring occasionally. Serve hot.

Spicy Version
You can spice this up by adding 1 tsp ground cumin, 1 tsp ground coriander and 1 small red chilli, deseeded and finely chopped (or ½ tsp dried chilli flakes) at the start, allowing the spices to sizzle in the pan for a minute before you add the onions.

Roast Squash with Chilli and Sage

It's easy to conjure up a lovely side dish from squash if you roast a tray of skin-on wedges with some harmonious flavourings muddled in. Being quite starchy and filling, it makes a great change from spuds. Leftovers are good cold too.

Serves 6

½ small squash (about 700g), deseeded and cut into wedges

3 large shallots or small red onions, cut into wedges

6–8 garlic cloves (unpeeled), bashed

2 tbsp olive or rapeseed oil

1 fairly mild medium-large red chilli, deseeded and sliced, or 1 tsp dried chilli flakes

12 sage leaves, or a few sprigs of rosemary

Sea salt and black pepper

Preheat the oven to 220°C/200°C Fan/Gas 7.

Put the squash wedges into an ovenproof dish with the shallots or onions and garlic. Trickle with the olive or rapeseed oil and season with salt and pepper.

Toss everything together and then spread the veg out evenly in the dish. Roast in the oven for 25 minutes until they are starting to colour nicely.

Take out the dish and toss the chilli and sage or rosemary through the veg, adding a dash more oil. Return to the oven for a further 10–15 minutes until everything is nicely roasted and the squash is caramelised at the edges.

Serve this side hot or at room temperature. The skin of the squash is quite edible but some varieties are a little tougher than others, so it's your call!

Additions

For a nutty, nutrient-rich addition and a zero-waste approach, pick the seeds from the squash pulp as you prepare the squash and add them in too, with the chilli and sage or rosemary. It's a labour of love to pick them out and crack open the shell to get to the seed inside. But tasty and satisfying if you have the patience!

You can also build this into a hearty veggie main course, by adding an eating apple or two, quartered, cored and cut into chunks, plus a couple of handfuls of walnuts, halfway through the roasting time.

Triple Treat Sides

Lemony Green Polenta

This pea-green wet polenta is a fantastic way to pack iron-rich greens into a simple side. The addition of lemon juice and zest just before serving keeps it wonderfully fresh, too. You can use any greens but it's great to combine spinach or chard with a brassica green, such as kale, cavolo nero or spring greens. This is so good, it also works as a starter as well as a side.

Serves 6–8

150g mixed greens, such as
  ½ kale and ½ spinach or chard,
  coarse stalks removed
4 tbsp extra virgin olive oil
2 garlic cloves, finely sliced or
  grated
50g crème fraîche, or soft ricotta
250g quick-cook polenta
A grating of lemon zest, plus
  a squeeze of juice
Sea salt and black pepper

Pour enough water into a medium saucepan to give a 3cm depth and bring to the boil. Add the greens, pushing them down with a spoon to make sure they are covered with the water and start to wilt. Bring back to a simmer and cook for just a minute, then drain in a colander and rinse under cold water. When cool enough to handle, squeeze the greens to remove excess water.

Put the wilted greens into a food processor with half of the extra virgin olive oil, the garlic and crème fraîche or ricotta. Pulse until the greens are finely chopped, but don't reduce them right down to a purée.

Cook the polenta in a pan of boiling water, according to the packet instructions (usually 1 part polenta to 4 parts water for around 5 minutes).

Once the polenta is cooked, stir through the creamy blitzed greens and heat through until piping hot. Taste to check the seasoning, adding salt and pepper to taste.

Serve the green polenta on warmed plates, topped with a final trickle of extra virgin olive oil, a grating of lemon zest and a squeeze of lemon juice.

This is a delicious accompaniment to roasted veg and saucy meat dishes, like my Slow-roast Merguez-spiced shoulder of lamb on page 140 or Sausage and lentils on page 139. It's also a great alternative to mash to serve with sausages, lamb chops or any grilled meat.

Vegan Green Polenta
Simply use Sunflower nut cream (page 220) or nut or oat milk in place of the crème fraîche or ricotta.

Sofrito Lentils

Lentils are a favourite in my kitchen, and while I love to have a tin of them to hand, sometimes they are best cooked from scratch. Here they are cooked with a 'sofrito' base of sweated onion, carrot and celery, which flavours the lentils beautifully, as well as boosting the plant count. You can serve the lentils warm or at room temperature, in which case they are especially good tossed with the mustardy dressing.

This recipe serves 8 and I would never make less, as they keep in the fridge for up to a week and are a fantastic asset to have on hand.

Serves 8

Oil or fat for cooking
1 tsp fennel or caraway seeds
  (optional)
2 medium onions, finely chopped
2–3 carrots, scrubbed or peeled
  and diced
2–3 celery sticks, diced
2 garlic cloves, sliced
A few sprigs of thyme
8 sage leaves or a sprig of
  rosemary (optional)
250g Puy lentils
A handful of parsley, leaves
  picked and roughly chopped
Sea salt and black pepper

Dressing (optional)

1 heaped tsp Dijon mustard
Juice of ½ lemon
3 tbsp extra virgin olive oil

Heat a little oil or fat in a large, wide pan over a medium-high heat. Once hot, add the fennel or caraway seeds if using and fry for a minute until fragrant and starting to crackle.

Add the onions, carrots, celery, garlic, thyme, sage or rosemary if using, and a pinch of salt. Sweat the veg uncovered, stirring often, for about 10 minutes until softened and golden.

Meanwhile, tip the lentils into a saucepan and cover with cold water. Bring to the boil, then immediately take off the heat and drain the lentils in a colander.

Once the veg are softened, add the blanched lentils and pour in 350ml cold water (it won't cover the lentils). Bring to a simmer then cover and cook gently for about 10 minutes, stirring often, until the lentils are tender but still with a slight nutty bite.

You will have a little liquor left in the pan at this stage. Drain this off if you want your lentils to be 'dry', or if you want to dress them; otherwise there's no need to – it's very tasty! Season with salt and pepper to taste and add a little more oil if you like.

To make the dressing, if required, put the ingredients into a screw-topped jar with some salt and pepper and shake until thick and creamy. Pour over the lentils and give it all a good stir.

Either way, finish the lentils with a scattering of chopped parsley.

Swaps and Additions

Replace or supplement the onions with sliced leeks, the carrots with diced parsnips or celeriac, and/or the celery with chopped fennel.
Or, for extra green veggie lentils, add 150g shredded leafy greens, such as chard, cavolo nero, kale or spinach (trimmed of coarse stalks). Stir into the lentils for the last 2 minutes of cooking. Leave to stand, covered, for 5 minutes to finish cooking in the residual heat. Stir again before serving.

Power Sprinkles, Plant Potions and Pickles

These very simple, versatile recipes can have a massive impact on the taste, goodness and visual appeal of your dishes, which is why I use the word 'power' to describe them. Whether it's a spoonful of nut and seed butter on your toast in the morning, a dollop of punchy pesto swirled into your soup, or a scoop of sauerkraut alongside supper, these ideas are superb for boosting flavour and, of course, they add immensely to your plant intake. Make a few, store them in your fridge or kitchen cupboard, and you'll have a little bit of extra plant magic at your fingertips.

These added-value extras include lots and lots of nuts, seeds, herbs and veg (and even a little fruit). You'll find them recommended alongside many dishes: the Sunflower and oat cream (page 220), for example, is great poured over my Beetroot and chocolate torte (on page 247) and equally delicious stirred into Shroomami stoup (page 54) or Roast squash and kale speltotto (on page 74). Similarly, the Nutty seedy clusters (page 204) complete a fantastic breakfast, with one of the fruit compotes on page 34 and a few spoonfuls of yoghurt, but also work as a straight-up snack.

This is one of the most diverse chapters in a very diverse book. In addition to recipes for seedy sprinkles, nut butters, hummus and pestos, there are a few pickles and raw ferments which add to the variety of plant foods you're eating.

Try my Golden glow sauerkraut (page 227), Purple-powered kim-kraut (page 228) or the lovely Carrot and apricot lacto-ferment (page 230). Ferments are particularly good for your gut biome because they deliver a dose of live, probiotic bacteria. These microbes give your digestive health a real boost by helping to build up the overall diversity of your gut biome. This is a welcome service at any time, but it is particularly useful if you are recovering from illness or if you have been taking antibiotics.

If you use raw cider vinegar with the live bacterial 'mother' in the bottle, for Giardiniera (page 223) and Cucumber quickle (page 224), they'll add to your probiotic intake too. In general, the best way to get the benefits of these 'live foods' is to eat them 'little and often', every day if it suits you. The pickle and ferment recipes here will keep in your fridge for weeks (if not months), meaning you'll have a good supply to hand, whenever you need it.

Once you have dabbled with a few of the recipes in this chapter you will find they are so darned handy at boosting your cooking – and your well-being – that you will find all kinds of ways to deploy them in your cooking. So, whether you're sprinkling or spooning, dunking or dipping, I know these recipes will add much more plant power to your elbow!

Nutty Seedy Clusters

Trail Mix

Crunchy Veg to Go

Toasted Tamari Seed Sprinkle

Dukka

Dot's Crackers

Nut and Seed Butter

Nutty Seedy Hummus

Seven-plant Pesto

Raita (and variations)

Sunflower and Oat Cream

Ajo Blanco Dressing

Giardiniera

Cucumber Quickle

Golden Glow Sauerkraut

Purple-powered Kim-kraut

Carrot and Apricot Lacto-ferment

Nutty Seedy Clusters

This is like an oatless granola, concentrating on the goodness of whole nuts and seeds, which can then be deployed in various ways – often, but not always, at breakfast time. It's brilliant sprinkled onto Multigrain porridge (page 31) or a plate of fruit (see page 28), or with either of the fruit compotes (on page 34) and yoghurt, but it can also be used to turbo-charge any breakfast cereal. The egg white helps 'clumping' but can be left out for a vegan version.

12–15 servings

200g pumpkin or sunflower
   seeds (or a mix)
30g whole flaxseed or chia seeds
   (or a mix)
30g poppy seeds (optional)
150g hazelnuts, almonds or
   walnuts (or a mix), roughly
   bashed
A generous pinch of salt
50ml rapeseed oil or melted
   coconut oil
30g soft brown sugar or
   1–1½ tbsp honey or maple
   syrup
1 medium egg white (optional)
100g mixed dried fruit (raisins,
   sultanas, chopped prunes and/
   or dried apricots (optional)

Preheat the oven to 190°C/170°C Fan/Gas 5. Line a large baking tray with baking paper.

Tip all of the seeds and the nuts into a large bowl, add the salt and stir to mix well.

Put the oil and sugar, honey or maple syrup into a small saucepan over a low heat and melt together, stirring gently, until smoothly combined and warm (not hot).

If using the egg white, whisk lightly in a small bowl until foamy.

Pour the warm oil and syrup mix over the seeds, add the egg white if using, and stir well until you have a damp, slightly sticky mixture. Pour onto the lined tray and spread out into an even layer.

Bake in the oven for 20–25 minutes until golden brown, giving the mix a couple of gentle stirs after about 10–15 minutes. Leave to cool completely and crisp up.

Once cooled, break up the nutty seedy sheet into pieces. You can mix the pieces with some dried fruit if you like (or simply add some when you serve up the clusters). They will keep in a jar or other airtight container for a couple of weeks.

Trail Mix

Barely a recipe, this is a simple assembly of nuts, seeds, dried fruit and a little dark chocolate: a multi-plant and mood-enhancing energy booster to keep your energy up when it's hard to make time for a proper meal. I often take a small tin of this and a larger one of Crunchy veg to go (below) when I'm working or travelling. Then I have a pretty balanced 'meal replacement' snack, and I've nailed at least 10 plants too!

2 snack-size servings

A small handful (about 20g) each of 3–4 of the following: pumpkin seeds, hazelnuts, walnuts, cashews, almonds, peanuts

A small handful (about 20g) each of 2 of the following: raisins or sultanas, dried cranberries or cherries, dried apricots (unsulphured), prunes, dried apple or pear

A few squares (about 30g) of dark chocolate

A pinch of fennel or caraway seeds (optional)

Put your pumpkin seeds, if using, and your chosen nuts into a small tin or plastic container.

Snip dried apricots and prunes, if using, into quarters and roughly chop the dried apple and/or pear. Break the dark chocolate into smaller pieces.

Add your chosen dried fruit, chocolate, and fennel or caraway seeds if using, to the tin and give it a shake.

Take with you when you travel or snack at your desk. Don't leave it in direct sunlight or too near a radiator! Eat within 24 hours.

Crunchy Veg to Go

When I'm travelling for work, especially on long train journeys, I like to have something like this with me. It keeps my energy levels up without spiking – and helps keep my eye off the snack trolley. It's worth making the time (10 minutes, tops) to prep it, pack it and take it with you. You'll always be glad you did.

1 serving

5 or more of the following:
1 carrot, scrubbed or peeled
½ small kohlrabi, peeled
¼ cucumber
1 or 2 inner sticks of celery
½ fennel bulb, trimmed
1 Little Gem lettuce heart, or a few inner leaves
½ apple
A few cherry tomatoes
Mint or basil leaves

Cut carrot, kohlrabi and cucumber into batons. Cut celery sticks into shorter lengths and fennel into thin wedges. Quarter the lettuce heart, if using. Core the apple and cut into chunky wedges.

Put all the prepared veg and fruit, and herb leaves if including, into a container suitable for travel and seal.

Eat the same day, ideally within 6 hours of preparing.

Toasted Tamari Seed Sprinkle

Sprinkling seeds into all kinds of dishes is generally an excellent idea and this is a simple way to make those seeds extra delicious, with a moreish umami glaze of tamari soy. Great for scattering over any kind of breakfast egg, bashed avocados, soups and salads, you'll see this sprinkle suggested as an optional extra in quite a few recipes.

Makes 1 small jar or 12 generous sprinkles

100g pumpkin seeds
100g sunflower seeds
3 tbsp tamari (or any other soy sauce you like)

Preheat the oven to 200°C/180°C Fan/Gas 6.

Mix the seeds and tamari together in a bowl, so all the seeds are coated, then tip onto a large, non-stick baking tray and spread out.

Toast in the oven for 10–12 minutes, taking the tray out to stir the seeds once or twice, until they are dark and there is no more liquid tamari visible.

As you remove the toasted seeds from the oven, give them a final stir, then leave to cool and dry on the tray. Once cooled, transfer to a jar, keep in a dark cupboard and use within 3 weeks.

Dukka

This is a simplified version of the classic Egyptian dukka – a trio of seeds toasted with a trio of seed spices. A sprinkle will boost the simplest of things, like a boiled egg, salad or steamed greens and it's a lovely crunchy finish for the hummus on page 214.

Makes 1 jar or 10–12 generous sprinkles

150g pumpkin seeds
100g sunflower seeds
50g sesame seeds (optional)
3 tsp cumin or caraway seeds
3 tsp coriander seeds
1 tsp fennel seeds (optional)
A good pinch of flaky sea salt
A few twists of black pepper
A small pinch of dried chilli flakes (optional)

Preheat the oven to 200°C/180°C Fan/Gas 6.

Scatter all the seeds and spices on a baking tray in a single, even layer. Toast in the oven for 8 minutes until lightly coloured and fragrant. Remove from the oven, tip onto a plate and leave to cool.

Using a pestle and mortar, lightly crush the seeds and spices, breaking them up rather than grinding them. (Or you can chop them on a board.) The idea is to roughen up the texture and release and mingle the flavours. It's no problem leaving a few whole seeds. Add the salt, pepper, and chilli flakes if using, and mix well.

You can use the dukka immediately, or store it in a jar or other airtight container for up to 2 weeks.

Nutty Dukka
Reduce the pumpkin and sunflower seeds by 50g each and replace with 100g hazelnuts, almonds or pistachios (or a mix). Scatter the nuts on a baking tray and toast for 5 minutes, then add all the other seeds and spices and return to the oven for 8 minutes. Bash or chop as above.

Dot's Crackers

Dot Sim is a friend of mine who lives on the Hebridean Island of Tiree making beautiful jewellery. She also often makes these fantastic crackers.

I like to top them with smashed avocado or a piece of cheese and a slice of apple. They are also great with pâté or hummus (see page 214), and delicious with honey or marmalade. They're handy to take as a snack when you are travelling too.

**Makes 10 large or
20 bite-sized crackers**

100g pumpkin seeds
75g sunflower seeds
50g chia seeds or flax seeds
   (or a mix)
30g sesame seeds or hemp
   seeds
50g fine plain wholemeal flour
A good pinch of salt
A twist of black pepper (optional)
2 tbsp extra virgin or rapeseed
   olive oil

Smashed avocado (optional)
1 ripe avocado
Finely grated zest and juice of
   ½ lemon
1 tbsp extra virgin olive or
   rapeseed oil
A pinch of dried chilli flakes
   (optional)

In a large bowl, mix all the seeds together thoroughly with the flour, adding the salt, and pepper if using. Now stir in 120ml water and the oil. Mix thoroughly until you have a sticky paste.

Leave the mixture to stand for at least 30 minutes, and up to an hour. This allows the chia and/or flax seeds to become gelatinous, which helps bind the paste.

Preheat the oven to 150°C/130°C Fan/Gas 2. Line a large baking sheet with baking paper.

Stir the mixture thoroughly again, adding another splash of water if it has become too stiff. Using a spatula, spread it evenly and thinly over the baking paper, as thinly as you can get it – to a 5mm thickness or less, ideally. Lay a second sheet of baking paper over the mixture and then flatten and smooth with your hand.

Place the tray in the centre of the oven and bake for an hour or so until golden brown and the seeds look toasted, turning the tray halfway through to ensure even cooking.

Carefully lift the cracker sheet on the paper onto a wire rack and leave to cool. Once cooled, break up the sheet into whatever sized pieces suits your purpose.

To make the smashed avocado topping, if required, in a bowl mash the avocado with the lemon zest and juice, extra virgin oil and some seasoning, keeping it quite chunky. Spread onto the crackers and top with a few chilli flakes if you like.

Swaps
You can play around with the seed mix, but the chia and flax seeds are helpful in creating a nice pasty mix that spreads well on the baking tray, so best to use at least one of these.

Gluten-free Crackers
Use cornflour, or a proprietary gluten-free baking flour, instead of the wholemeal flour.

Nut and Seed Butter

This is well worth making for its sheer versatility, as well as the pleasure of having it straight up on (wholegrain) toast. I like to make it with half raw, half toasted nuts and seeds, as I think this gives the best balance of flavour and goodness. You'll see that I use this nutrient-rich butter in other things too, like my Nutty seedy hummus (overleaf), and you can use it whenever a nut butter is called for in a recipe.

Makes 2 small jars

500g mixed nuts, such as
  almonds, hazelnuts, cashews,
  pistachios, macadamia nuts and
  peanuts (at least 2 types)
250g pumpkin or sunflower
  seeds (or a mix)
1 tsp ground cinnamon (optional)
A small pinch of salt (optional)

Preheat the oven to 200°C/180°C Fan/Gas 6.

Scatter roughly half of your chosen nuts and seeds on a baking tray in a single layer. Toast in the oven for 8–10 minutes until lightly coloured. Allow to cool completely.

If you want a chunky nut butter, set aside about 50g of the toasted nuts to add back in later.

Aside from that, put all the seeds and nuts, both raw and toasted, into a food processor, with the ground cinnamon and salt if using. Blitz for 4–6 minutes, stopping to scrape down the sides every so often. It takes a while for the oils to be released and the nut butter to become silky and smooth.

At this point, add in whole nuts and seeds reserved for a chunky butter and pulse a few times until they are roughly chopped into the butter.

Spoon the nut and seed butter into clean jars. It will keep in the fridge for up to 3 months.

You can spread the butter on toast, oatcakes or a slice of porridge bread (page 46). Or dab it onto pancakes (see page 36) or serve it with sliced apples and other fruits for dipping (see page 28).

Swaps and Additions
For a lovely double dose of nuts and seeds, try topping the nut and seed butter with Toasted tamari seed sprinkle or Dukka (page 209).

Nutty Seedy Hummus

Hummus is such a handy thing to have on standby in the fridge for healthy snacks and simple lunch(box)es. This version piles in some soaked seeds and nuts for extra texture, and plenty of lemon zest and juice. I often swap nut butter for the traditional tahini, too.

I'm still a big fan of serving up a bowl of hummus with some crunchy seasonal veg for dipping in. But don't just stop at carrots, cucumber and celery – think also of fennel, radishes, kohlrabi, baby courgettes, cauliflower florets and wedges of radicchio, chicory or Little Gem lettuce. If I'm serving some cucumber batons, I like to scrape out the wet, jelly-like seeds and blitz them into the hummus.

Loosened with a little water, hummus is a great dressing for salads, kebabs and my Slow-roast Merguez-spiced shoulder of lamb (page 140).

Serves 4

75g skin-on almonds, or cashew nuts
100g mixed seeds, such as sunflower, pumpkin, sesame and linseed
400g tin chickpeas
Seedy middle of ½ cucumber (optional, see above)
100ml extra virgin olive, rapeseed or hempseed oil, plus extra to finish
Finely grated zest and juice of ½–1 lemon
½ garlic clove, finely grated or crushed
2 tbsp Nut and seed butter (see page 213), or tahini
Sea salt and black pepper

To finish and serve
A pinch of paprika (optional)
Dukka (page 209, optional)
A selection of raw vegetables, cut into sticks or wedges as appropriate
Dot's crackers (page 210, optional)

Put the almonds or cashews and mixed seeds into a bowl and cover with plenty of cold water. Leave to soak in the fridge for at least 3 hours, or overnight (they will swell and expand a little).

Drain the chickpeas, reserving 4 tbsp of the liquid from the tin.

Drain the nuts and seeds and tip them into a food processor with the chickpeas. Add some salt and pepper, and the seedy cucumber if using. Blitz until the nuts and seeds are well chopped.

Now, with the motor running, gradually trickle in the extra virgin oil, stopping to scrape down the sides of the bowl once or twice so it blends evenly.

Add the lemon zest and juice, garlic and nut and seed butter or tahini and pulse again, trickling in enough of the reserved chickpea water to create a creamy but slightly textured purée.

Scoop the hummus out into a serving bowl. Top with a final swirl of extra virgin oil, a pinch of paprika and/or a sprinkling of dukka if you like. Serve up with plenty of crunchy seasonal vegetables for dipping, and crackers if you like.

Power Sprinkles, Plant Potions and Pickles

Seven-plant Pesto

I've been making endless variations on the pesto theme for years now – there are so many fun combinations of nuts, seeds, herbs, greens and oils to try. I often leave out the cheese, as it's easy to add later. This is a great all-rounder, with a bunch of fun swaps and a lovely nettle and wild garlic variation below.

Pesto is great tossed through wholegrain pasta, or boiled new potatoes, and it's a brilliant way to finish various soups and salads too. I also love it spread generously on wholegrain toast under a couple of poached or scrambled eggs.

Makes a 350ml jar

50g hazelnuts or walnuts
50g pumpkin seeds
100g baby spinach
A large bunch of parsley
  (50–70g), leaves picked
¼ garlic clove
50g Cheddar or Parmesan,
  finely grated (optional)
Finely grated zest and juice
  of ½ lemon, or to taste
Up to 150ml extra virgin
  rapeseed oil
Sea salt and black pepper

Lightly toast the nuts and seeds in a dry frying pan for a few minutes then tip onto a plate to cool.

Put the spinach, parsley, garlic and toasted nuts and seeds into a food processor and blitz until chopped, but still retaining some texture. Add the grated cheese if using, plus the lemon zest and juice, and pulse to mix through.

Now begin trickling in the extra virgin oil, pulsing the processor as you do so. Stop blitzing when you have a loose but still pleasingly granular texture with flecks of spinach and parsley still visible. You can add more oil to loosen the pesto once you are happy with the texture of the nuts, seeds and greens. Taste and add salt, pepper and more lemon juice if you like.

Transfer any pesto you're not serving straight away to a jar, cover the surface with a layer of oil and store in the fridge until needed. It will keep in the fridge (topped with oil) for up to a month.

Swaps
Feel free to vary your combinations of greens, herbs, nuts, seeds and oils:
Nuts Try cashews, almonds, peanuts, pine nuts and pistachios, either on their own or in combination.
Seeds Swap in sunflower seeds or hulled hemp seed.
Greens Use watercress, rocket or kale in place of, or as well as, spinach.
Herbs Use basil or nasturtium leaves instead of (or in with) the parsley.
Oils Swap in olive, hemp, sunflower or pumpkin seed oil.
And if you use 3 greens or herbs, 3 nuts or seeds and a pair of oils, plus garlic, pepper and salt, you'll push your plant count into double figures.

Nettle and Wild Garlic Pesto
For a lovely seasonal variation, in early spring replace the spinach with young nettle tops and use wild garlic leaves instead of (or as well as) the parsley. First blanch the nettle tops for 30 seconds, then drain, refresh and squeeze as dry as you can, before making the pesto.

Raita

Raita is delicious served up with a curry, and a lovely way to finish a spicy soup, but it can accompany other dishes too. As well as cucumber, mint and garlic, I like to get a bit of spice in, and at least one other veg. Celery works well, but you can also take your cue from the dish you are serving it with. For example, I like to add some grated raw squash when I'm serving the raita with spicy squash dishes, like the Squash mulligatawny on page 58. And I've suggested a courgette version for the meatballs on page 145 too.

Serves x

½ medium cucumber
 (about 200g)
2 inner sticks of celery
A scrap of garlic (no more than
 ¼ clove)
½ tsp cumin or caraway seeds,
 bashed
200ml whole natural (or plant-
 based) yoghurt
1–2 tbsp mint leaves
1–2 tbsp finely chopped parsley
Sea salt and black pepper

Coarsely grate the cucumber, then squeeze in your hands to remove some of the liquid before placing in a bowl. Thinly slice the celery and add to the bowl. Grate or crush the garlic and mash with a small pinch of salt. Add to the cucumber and celery, along with the spice seeds and yoghurt, and mix well together.

Slice the mint into fine ribbons and stir through the yoghurt mix, along with the chopped parsley. If you have time, leave to stand for 20 minutes or so, then stir the raita again before serving.

Swaps and Additions
Veg A small, firm courgette works well instead of the cucumber. In place of the celery, you can use 6 radishes, a small fennel bulb or ½ small kohlrabi (about 100g), either finely sliced or coarsely grated. A small wedge of raw squash (about 100g), grated, is a fun and colourful addition to the raita, especially when you're serving it with a squash dish.
Herbs Chopped coriander, lovage, chervil, tarragon or chives (or any combination of these), can be used instead of, or as well as, the parsley.
Coconut Scatter 150g desiccated coconut in a small ovenproof dish and toast in a preheated oven at 180°C/160°C Fan/Gas 4 for about 10 minutes until golden, then tip into a bowl and leave to cool. Once cooled, add 2 tbsp hot water and leave to soak for 5 minutes. Stir the coconut through the raita.

Sunflower and Oat Cream

This is a brilliant recipe for a simple vegan alternative to dairy cream, and you don't have to be vegan to enjoy it. It's great to serve with any dessert where a trickle of cream is the treat you want to finish it off – for example a crumble (see page 234), the Beetroot and chocolate torte on page 247, or a simple bowl of lovely summer berries.

It's handy in a savoury context too, for example trickled into soups like my Shroomami stoup (page 54) instead of yoghurt or dairy cream. And I like to use it to enrich my Roast squash and kale speltotto with rosemary (page 74).

It certainly helps to have a powerful high-speed blender to get a properly creamy consistency, but if yours is not quite so punchy, just blitz for a good 5 minutes then pass your cream through a fine sieve.

Makes about 500ml

75g sunflower seeds
50g oats (porridge or jumbo)
2 tbsp extra virgin rapeseed oil
  (optional)

Put the sunflower seeds and oats into a bowl or jar, cover with 350ml cold water and stir well. Place in the fridge and leave to soak for at least 3 hours or overnight. (It's important to keep it cold so it doesn't start to ferment.)

Tip the mixture into a blender. For an even richer, creamier version add the extra virgin rapeseed oil now. Blitz on maximum speed for at least a minute, and up to 5 minutes, until thick, creamy and really smooth. It should be spoonable, almost like double cream.

If you would like it thinner and pourable (more like single cream), just add a splash more water and blitz again.

Pour into a clean container, seal and refrigerate until needed. It will keep for up to a week in the fridge; it is likely to separate but can easily be whisked back together with a fork.

Swaps
Replace from around half up to all of the sunflower seeds with cashews, almonds or even hazelnuts for a richer, nuttier, slightly sweeter flavour. Just make sure you give them all a good soak for maximum creaminess.

Sunflower and Oat Milk
For a great all-round plant milk, keep adding more cold water as you blitz, about 800–900ml in total, until the consistency is just a little thicker than ordinary milk.

Ajo Blanco Dressing

Ajo blanco is traditionally a Spanish almond-based soup. Here I'm using similar ingredients to make a creamy, nutty, lemony dressing – a lovely idea from my chef friend Lulu Cox.

It works particularly well on the raw kale and squash salad (on page 106), but is very versatile. Once you've made it, I'm sure you will enjoy trying it on all kinds of salads and slaws, and also trickling it over trays of roast veg. If you make it first up for the kale and squash, you'll have enough left over to try out on other salads too.

Makes about 350ml

125g almonds or hazelnuts
175ml nut or oat milk (home-
  made version opposite)
½ garlic clove, roughly chopped
Finely grated zest and juice of
  ½ lemon
100ml extra virgin olive oil
Sea salt and black pepper

To make the dressing, put the nuts, plant milk, garlic and lemon zest and juice into a blender and blitz until fairly smooth.

Now, with the motor running, trickle in the extra virgin olive oil. The dressing will thicken and emulsify; if it's a bit thick once you've added all the oil, add a little water to thin it. Season the dressing with salt and pepper, and more lemon juice if you think it needs it.

Keep the dressing in the sealed jar in the fridge until needed, then shake vigorously to re-emulsify before using. It will keep, chilled, for about a week.

Swaps and Additions
By all means experiment with different nuts, seeds and cold-pressed oils (such as rapeseed or hempseed). And you can use vinegar (such as live cider vinegar) instead of the lemon zest and juice. The flavours may change considerably, but every version will have its merits.

Giardiniera

The direct translation of this Italian-style pickle is 'gardener', based on the principle that you can pretty much pack your veg patch into this pickle. Another name for the medley is 'sottaceti', which means 'under vinegar' and alludes to the pickling medium. It gives the veg a sharp yet delicious tang.

This is one of the simplest and healthiest methods for making a pickle – with raw veg and an unheated raw cider vinegar brine, as it retains the goodness of both the veg and the vinegar. If you can source raw apple cider vinegar with the mother, even better. I've used one very large jar, but you may prefer to pack the pickle into two 1 litre jars.

Makes 1 very large (2 litre) jar or 2 x 1 litre jars

1 small cauliflower (500–600g)
1 small fennel bulb, trimmed, or 2–3 celery sticks (100g)
1 small courgette (100g), trimmed
A fistful of runner or green (French) beans (100g), trimmed
1 red, yellow or green pepper (100g), halved, cored and deseeded
1 medium carrot (100g), scrubbed or peeled
3 tbsp sea salt
3 garlic cloves
3 bay leaves
1 tsp fennel seeds
1 tsp coriander seeds
1 tsp black peppercorns
3 small red or green chillies, or 3 pinches of dried chilli flakes (optional)
750ml apple cider vinegar (ideally raw, see above)

Cut all of the veg (except the chillies) into bite-sized pieces, place in a large bowl and sprinkle with the sea salt. Toss to mix well. Cover with a clean cloth and leave in a cool place for at least 2 hours or overnight – this will draw out excess moisture from the veg, which will help keep your pickle crisp.

In the meantime, sterilise a 2 litre or 2 x 1 litre preserving jar(s) with vinegar-proof lid(s) (see below) and allow to cool.

After salting, tip the veg into a colander and rinse under cold water. Allow to drain.

Pack the sterilised jar(s) half-full with veg. Crush each garlic clove with the flat of a knife to gently 'crack' it. Tuck the 'cracked' garlic cloves and bay leaves into the jar(s).

Mix the fennel and coriander seeds and the peppercorns together in a small bowl then add to the jar(s). For a spicy pickle, add the chillies or chilli flakes, too.

Fill the jar(s) with the remaining veg. In a jug, whisk the apple cider vinegar with 250ml water. Pour this liquid over the veg in the jar(s), filling to the brim. Seal the jar(s) with a lid and leave to mature for at least a week before eating.

The pickle will keep in a cool, dark cupboard for up to 6 months. Refrigerate once opened and eat within a month.

To Sterilise Jars
Heat the oven to 100°C/Fan 80°C/Gas ¼. Thoroughly wash the jars and lids in hot soapy water. Stand the jars in an ovenproof dish, making sure they are not touching each other. Put into the oven for 10 minutes. To sterilise the lids, immerse them in a pan of boiling water for the same amount of time then place on a clean tea towel to drain. Take the jars out of the oven and let cool; or fill them while they are still hot if you're packing a hot pickle into them.

Cucumber Quickle

This is a delightful quick pickle of cucumber with some nice crunchy companions. Dill is the classic aromatic, but you can easily swap it out for mint or tarragon if either is closer to hand. Or you can use dried dill in the colder months.

The great thing about a quickle is that you don't have to wait to tuck in! It's like a tangy crunchy salad, dressed only with vinegar, no oil. It makes a juicy contrast to many dishes, including fish and meat – it's lovely with grilled mackerel or roast chicken. It is also good with pulses – try it with my Sofrito lentils (page 200).

Serves 4

2 small or 1 large cucumber (about 250g)

1 small or ½ large fennel bulb (about 100g), trimmed, or 2 inner sticks of celery

5–6 radishes (optional)

1 small eating apple

100g grapes (optional)

3 spring onions, trimmed and thinly sliced

1 tsp coriander seeds

1 tsp sea salt

2 tbsp apple cider vinegar (ideally raw, with the mother if possible)

A small bunch of dill (or fennel fronds) or mint, or 1 tbsp dried dill or tarragon

Cut the cucumber into 5mm–1cm rounds. Thinly slice the fennel or celery into 5mm slices on the diagonal (and chop the fronds to include, too, if you have them). Thinly slice the radishes, if using.

Cut the apple into 1cm dice, discarding the core but keeping the skin on. Halve and de-pip the grapes if using.

Place these prepared veg and fruit in a shallow bowl, along with the spring onions. Sprinkle over the coriander seeds and salt and toss well. Leave to stand for 15 minutes, to draw out some liquid from the fruit and veg.

Sprinkle the apple cider vinegar over the veg and fruit mix. Finely chop the dill or mint if using and add to the pickle, or sprinkle in the dried dill or tarragon. Fold through and leave to macerate for 30 minutes, then toss again.

You can eat this quickle straight away or transfer it to a lidded container and store it in the fridge for up to 3 days.

Golden Glow Sauerkraut

Sauerkrauts are a great way of combining some lovely veg, while also serving them up with the biome-benefiting bacteria that come with this age-old technique of preserving through fermentation.

This is one of my favourite all-rounder sauerkrauts, which turns brassicas and roots into a sunny golden kraut with a lovely tang of fresh turmeric and ginger. It's an excellent way to give yourself a seasonal vitamin C boost too, as fermented veg can make up to 50 per cent more vitamin C available than simply munching them raw.

Makes 1 large (1.5 litre) jar

1 medium white cabbage
  (800–900g)
½ medium celeriac, peeled, or
  2 medium turnips, scrubbed
  (about 250g)
3 large carrots, scrubbed or
  peeled (about 250g)
1 garlic clove, peeled and finely
  grated
5cm piece of fresh ginger, finely
  grated (no need to peel)
5cm piece of fresh turmeric,
  finely grated (no need to peel),
  or 2 tsp ground
2 tsp cumin or caraway seeds
  (or 1 tsp of each)
1 tsp thyme leaves (optional)
A few twists of black pepper
About 25g sea salt

Thoroughly wash and dry a large 1.5 litre preserving jar (I use a Kilner jar). Strip 2 outer leaves from your cabbage and set aside.

Finely shred the rest of the cabbage and place in a large non-metallic bowl. (Finely slice or grate the thicker leaf spines and central core, rather than discard them.) Coarsely grate the celeriac or turnips and carrots. Add the garlic, ginger and turmeric to the veg, with the cumin or caraway seeds, thyme if using, and pepper.

Weigh the mixture. Calculate 2% sea salt; i.e. for every 100g prepared veg, you want 2g sea salt. Add the salt to the veg mix and massage it in with your (very clean!) hands. After a minute or two, liquid will start to be released from the veg. Keep massaging and squeezing the veg until there is a good pool of briney liquid in the bottom of the bowl.

Spoon the briney veg mixture into the preserving jar a few handfuls at a time, packing down each layer; more brine should be released as you go. You want the kraut to fill the jar to the line just below where the lid sits, leaving at least 2cm space at the top.

Lay the saved cabbage leaves on top and press to hold the veg/fruit mixture down. If the mixture has not created enough brine to comfortably cover the kraut, add a pinch of salt and top up above the cabbage leaves with cold water. (You can also use a washed pebble or non-metallic weight to keep the kraut under the brine.)

Close the lid of the jar but not too tightly, so that fermenting gases can bubble out (I remove the rubber seal from the jar to facilitate this). Stand the jar on a plate or tray to catch any juices that might bubble out during the fermentation process. Leave to ferment at cool room temperature for 10–14 days until the kraut is pleasantly tangy and tender.

Once fermented, transfer the jar to the fridge, where the kraut will keep for up to 3 months if the veg is submerged. I put some kind of sauerkraut on the table several times a week, and there's almost no meal for which I consider it inappropriate to do so.

Purple-powered Kim-kraut

This completes my trio of 'purple power' recipes, the others being Purple shakshuka (page 42) and Purple panzanella (page 98). I'm grateful to my friend and River Cottage fermentation guru Rachel de Thample for helping me knock this one into shape.

The process is identical to the previous recipe, with a different set of ingredients giving a very different character and a nice hit of chilli lending the powerful punch of a Korean kimchi, though I would never claim this is an authentic kimchi! The prunes are a surprising addition, which contrasts nicely with the bitter note of radicchio. The latter is very distinctive, and may not be to everyone's taste (though I love it). If you don't fancy it, just up the cabbage to replace.

Makes 1 large (1.5 litre) jar

1 medium or ½ large red
   cabbage (about 600g)
1 radicchio or purple/red chicory
   bulb (about 200g), or an extra
   200g cabbage
1 large or 2 medium beetroot
   (about 200g)
1 small red onion (about 100g),
   thinly sliced
1 tbsp finely grated fresh ginger
2 garlic cloves, finely grated
1 medium-hot red chilli, finely
   sliced, or 1 tsp dried chilli flakes
1 tbsp sweet paprika
50g pitted prunes, sliced
About 20g sea salt
2 cabbage leaves

Thoroughly wash and dry a large 1.5 litre preserving jar with an airtight lid. Strip 2 outer leaves from the cabbage, to cover your kraut, and set aside.

Finely shred the cabbage. Slice the radicchio or chicory, if using, into 2–3cm wide ribbons. Give the beetroot a good scrub (no need to peel – this is where a lot of the good bacteria and nutrients are) then coarsely grate it. Put these prepared veg into a large non-metallic bowl with the onion. Add the ginger, garlic, chilli, paprika and prunes to the bowl and mix thoroughly with the veg.

Weigh the mixture and calculate 2g sea salt for every 100g veg. Add the salt to the veg mix and massage it in with your hands. After a minute or two, liquid will start to be released from the veg. Keep massaging and squeezing the veg until there is a good pool of briney liquid in the bottom of the bowl.

Spoon the briney veg mixture into the preserving jar a few handfuls at a time, packing down each layer; more brine should be released as you go. You want the kraut to fill the jar to the line just below where the lid sits, leaving at least 2cm space at the top.

Lay the saved cabbage leaves on top and press to hold the veg/fruit mixture down. If the mixture has not created enough brine to comfortably cover the kraut, add a pinch of salt and top up above the cabbage leaves with cold water. (You can also use a washed pebble or non-metallic weight to keep the kraut under the brine.)

Close the lid but not too tightly (remove the rubber seal), so that fermenting gases can bubble out. Stand the jar on a plate or tray to catch any juices that might bubble out during fermentation.

Leave to ferment at cool room temperature for 10–14 days until the kraut tastes pleasantly tangy. Store in the fridge thereafter. It will keep for 3 months, provided the veg is submerged in brine.

Carrot and Apricot Lacto-ferment

This bright orange pickle is a great combination of sweet and sour flavours. It's called a 'lacto-ferment', because during the process lactic acid is released, which inhibits the growth of harmful bacteria. It's all about the 4 per cent brine, with which you can cover any number of veg, spices and fruits to ferment. The technique is ideal for chunky pickles, as opposed to krauts using shredded veg. This one is delicious alongside roasted veg, the sausage and lentils on page 139, or with any leftover meat or cheese.

Makes 1 large (1.5 litre) jar

40g salt
600g medium-large carrots,
  peeled or scrubbed
250g dried apricots
  (unsulphured)
1-2 chillies (ideally large and
  fairly mild)
A large knob of fresh ginger
  (30–40g)
2 tsp coriander seeds

Thoroughly wash a 1.5 litre storage jar and rinse well. Tip the salt into a large measuring jug (at least 1 litre capacity) and add about 200ml boiling water from the kettle. Stir well to dissolve most of the salt (it doesn't have to be fully dissolved). Top up to 1 litre with fresh cold water and stir until all of the salt is dissolved.

Halve the carrots lengthways, then slice on an angle into short (5cm) batons. Snip or slice the apricots into halves. Finely slice the chillies. There's no need to peel the ginger, but trim off any tired bits, give it a wash and slice as thinly as you can.

Pile the carrots, apricots, chillies and ginger into the jar, mingling them and sprinkling in a few coriander seeds as you go. Pour on the brine so everything is completely covered (you might not need it all). If any veg are inclined to float, use a well-washed pebble or small clean jar that fits inside the big one, to weigh it down.

Place the jar on a tray to catch any liquid that bubbles over. Put the lid on and leave to ferment at room temperature.

Once there are signs of bubbling and burping, it will take another week or so for the pickle to be ready. Taste for acidity, and if you like it, transfer the jar to the fridge where the process will slow right down. If you like it tangy, leave at room temperature for another week or more. Once opened, refrigerate and eat within 1 month.

Crunchy Summer Pickle
Use 300g each of radishes, halved lengthways, cauliflower in small florets (or wedges of kohlrabi), and baby carrots, scrubbed and quartered lengthways with a bit of the green leaf still on. Season with 1 tsp each of coriander, caraway and cumin seeds, plus a few twists of black pepper.

Autumn Roots and Fruits Pickle
Use 250g each of carrot (or parsnip) and swede (or celeriac) in chunky batons, 1 small onion, sliced, and 2 medium crisp eating apples (skin on), cored and cut into wedges. Season with 1 tsp each of caraway (or fennel) and coriander seeds.

Power Sprinkles, Plant Potions and Pickles

Multi-plant Puds and Treats

This chapter proves that sweet treats are not inherently 'bad for you'. Far from it. Provided you pack your puds and bakes full of good things, they can make a genuinely positive contribution to your daily nutrition. Those things may include eggs, and a little dairy produce. But it will be no surprise to you by now that, mostly, they'll be plants. And we'll see that the plants that most lend themselves to this mission are fruits, nuts and seeds – with a few surprising vegetables thrown in.

From a lemon cake featuring grated courgettes, ground nuts and poppy seeds (on page 256) to a citrusy, prune-speckled spotted Dick (on page 238), all the recipes are not only delectable, they definitely deliver on plants. They will grant your wish for something on the sweet side, with the advantage of being very satisfying as well.

Recipes that are high in sugar and other refined carbs, like white flour, can cause energy spikes and crashes, leading to fluctuations of mood and unhelpful cravings. But if you dial down the sugar you are using and mingle it with whole foods like nuts, fruits and seeds, and wholegrain flours too, then you can mitigate these spikes by offering dishes that are richer in plant proteins and fibre, and therefore release their energy over a longer period. You'll find them just as irresistible as old-school versions, but much more satisfying.

Take my Nutty seedy frangipane tart (page 253), for instance: it uses a little sugar but there are also lots of almonds, pumpkin and poppy seeds in it, and the recipe can be easily adapted to be baked with fruit or without. And it's not only the frangipane filling that's had a multi-plant upgrade: the hob-nobby, half-wholemeal shortcrust pastry is also packed with good things.

You'll also find a gorgeous pair of fruity, yoghurt-based ice creams – a welcome treat for the summer holidays and beyond that will delight the whole family, especially kids. The Tutti-frutti semifreddo (on page 243) is naturally sweetened with ripe banana, and studded with tangy dried fruits and zesty citrus peel, and the Very berry fro-yo (on page 244)… well, it speaks for itself.

Foods that are flexible are one of the keys to plant-ful eating, hence my 'wholed-up' classic crumble (on page 234), with oats, nuts and seeds. It's baked separately so it can be deployed with many different fruits, both fresh and stewed, for a pleasing variety of possible outcomes – depending on the season and what you have to hand. Similarly, my cookie recipe is cunningly customisable: I suggest you try the Chocolate and spice cookies (page 261) first, but any number of dried fruits, nuts and seeds can be introduced, to ring the changes and rack up the plant count.

I know people can be sceptical of the mission to make our favourite foods 'healthy'. And so I have gone to considerable lengths to make sure the collection in this chapter really delivers. The recipes are carefully calibrated and painstakingly put together. Above all they have been tested and tweaked several times over until they consistently delight the most demanding palates: those of my own family and friends.

It is a particular source of pride to have such a dependable repertoire of plant-packed treats and puds at my disposal. And now it is a real pleasure for me to put it at yours.

Multifruit Multigrain Crumbles

Very Spotted Dick

Tutti-frutti Semifreddo

Very Berry Ripple Fro-yo

Beetroot and Chocolate Torte

Hob-nobby Shortcrust Pastry

Nutty Seedy Frangipane Tart

Courgette, Honey and Lemon Cake

Maple and Nut Butter Flapjacks

Chocolate and Spice Cookies

Multifruit Multigrain Crumbles

You can certainly pack a lot of plants and all-round goodness into a crumble. Once you've made your crumble you can pile it on top of a fruit base and bake it straight away for a classic baked crumble. Or, you can bake it on its own and keep it handy to use whenever you need a pud. I love the practicality of this.

The joy of the pre-baked crumble is that it can turn any juicy, fruity combination – both raw and cooked – into a delicious, wholesome pud. Try my suggestions below and overleaf.

Swirl some yoghurt, or half yoghurt/half whipped cream, with the fruit before you top it with the crumble and you have yourself a fumble – a cross between a fool and a crumble.

Crumble

15–20 servings

100g fine plain wholemeal flour
100g porridge oats
100g ground almonds or
   hazelnuts
50g soft light brown sugar
A pinch of salt
150g cold butter, diced, or
   120g chilled coconut oil
50g pumpkin or sunflower seeds
   (or a mix)
50g hazelnuts, roughly chopped,
   or flaked almonds

Preheat the oven to 200°C/180°C/Gas 6.

In a large bowl, mix the flour, oats, ground nuts, sugar and salt together until evenly combined. Tip in the diced butter and rub into the dry ingredients using your fingertips until the mixture becomes crumbly. Finally mix in the seeds and nuts.

Squeeze the crumble mix into clumps in your hands, then crumble these onto a baking tray, so you have pieces of various shapes and size. Bake for 25–30 minutes, taking the tray out halfway through to give the crumble a good stir. It's ready when it's nice and golden – a little darker in some parts than others. Give it another stir when you take it out, then leave to cool completely on the tray.

Store the crumble in an airtight container for up to 2 weeks. Allow around 2 tablespoonfuls per serving.

Macerated Summer Berries

Serves 5–6

500g mixed berries, such as
   strawberries, raspberries,
   blackberries, blueberries
   and/or red- or white currants
   (ideally at least two)
Finely grated zest and juice of
   1 lemon
30–50g golden caster sugar
Thick yoghurt, or half yoghurt/
   half whipped cream (optional)

Put all the berries into a bowl with the lemon zest and juice and 30g sugar and toss together lightly. Leave to macerate for up to an hour, gently turning the berries occasionally to release their juices. Taste, and, if the berries are very tart, mix in just a little more sugar.

Pile the berries into bowls or glasses, swirl with a dash of yoghurt and or/cream if you like (for the fumble version) and serve generously topped with the pre-baked crumble.

Continued overleaf

Multi-plant Puds and Treats

St Clements Apple and Pear Compote

Serves 5–6

4–5 medium eating apples,
  such as Cox or Braeburn
2–3 firm pears
30g soft light brown sugar
Finely grated zest and juice of
  2 oranges
Finely grated zest and juice of
  1 lemon
2cm piece of fresh ginger, thinly
  sliced (optional)

Quarter, core and slice the apples and pears into 1–2 cm thick wedges. Place in a medium saucepan with the sugar, orange and lemon zest and juice, and the ginger if using. Add a little water to just cover the fruit if needed. Bring to a low simmer and poach very gently for 6–8 minutes until the fruit is tender but holding its shape.

Using a slotted spoon, transfer the apples and pears to a bowl. Briskly boil the juice for a few minutes to reduce and thicken slightly (or boil for longer to get a thicker syrup if you like). Pour the syrup back over the apples and pears and leave to cool.

Serve the fruit with a trickle of the syrup and the pre-baked crumble (from page 234), with a bowl of yoghurt on the side if you like.

Other Fruity Compotes

Bramley Apple

Use Bramleys or other cooking apples in the recipe above instead of, or in combination with, the 'eating' apples. Peel, core and thinly slice Bramleys – they will collapse to a purée on cooking, to make a luscious golden apple compote, with the pear and/or eating apple pieces adding texture.

Gooseberry and Elderflower

Poach 700g gooseberries in just a trickle of water with a few fresh elderflower heads and about 50g sugar (a little more if they are very tart). Simmer gently so the gooseberries burst and the juice runs, until you have a tender compote. Leave to cool then remove the elderflower before serving.

Rhubarb and Orange

Cut 700g rhubarb into 4–5cm lengths and place in an ovenproof dish in a single layer. Sprinkle with 50g caster sugar and the grated zest and juice of 1 orange. Bake at 200°C/180°C Fan/Gas 6 for about 15 minutes until just tender. Transfer to a bowl with all the juices in the dish and leave to cool.

Plum, Ginger and Star Anise

Halve 1kg plums and remove the stones. Arrange the plums in a layer in an ovenproof dish, and scatter over some thinly sliced fresh ginger, a couple of bashed star anise and about 70g caster sugar. Bake at 200°C/180°C Fan/Gas 6 for about 35 minutes, stirring gently halfway through, until the plums are tender. Transfer to a bowl with all the juices and leave to cool.

Very Spotted Dick

A steamed pudding is a classic comfort pud, but there is absolutely no reason not to customise it with a variety of fruits and even some nuts and oats. More plants means more goodness – and more delicious spots in the Dick!

See overleaf for my festive variation: a lighter version of a classic Christmas pud.

Serves 6–8

150g butter, softened, plus extra
  to grease the basin
50g raisins
50g dried prunes or apricots
  (unsulphured), roughly chopped
1 tsp ground ginger or 1cm piece
  of fresh ginger, grated
100g fine plain wholemeal flour
30g ground almonds
40g porridge oats
20g poppy seeds
2 level tsp baking powder
A pinch of salt
75g golden caster sugar or
  soft brown sugar
Finely grated zest of 2 lemons
  and juice of 1 lemon
Finely grated zest of 1 orange
3 medium eggs

Lemony ginger topping
Juice of 2 lemons (use the other
  zested lemon from above)
4 tbsp soft dark brown sugar
3cm piece of fresh ginger, grated

To serve
Cream, yoghurt, crème fraîche
  or Sunflower and oat cream
  (page 220)

Grease an 850ml capacity pudding basin with a little butter. Cut a double layer of foil or baking paper that will generously cover the top of the pudding basin (with plenty of overhang) and butter one layer of this too; set aside.

For the lemony ginger topping, in a small bowl stir together the lemon juice, brown sugar and ginger until well blended (don't worry if the sugar doesn't fully dissolve). Tip this mixture into the pudding basin.

For the filling, toss the raisins and prunes or apricots with 1 tbsp of the flour and set aside (the flour coating helps to stop the raisins sinking as the pudding cooks).

Tip the rest of the flour into a bowl and add the ground almonds, oats, poppy seeds, baking powder and pinch of salt. Toss to mix and set aside.

Put the butter, sugar and lemon and orange zest into a large bowl or the bowl of a stand mixer. Using an electric hand mixer or the stand mixer, beat together until light and fluffy. Add 1 egg, with a spoonful of the flour mix, and beat in. Repeat to incorporate the other 2 eggs.

Now tip the flour, almond and oat mix into the mixture and use a large spoon to fold it in lightly but thoroughly. Add the lemon juice and fold through, then finally, gently fold in the floured raisins and prunes or apricots.

Spoon the mixture carefully into the pudding basin (the lemony ginger topping in the bottom will rise up the sides; don't worry about this).

Make a pleat in the centre of the doubled foil or paper and lay, buttered side down, over the basin. (The pleat will allow room for the pudding to expand during cooking.) Secure with kitchen string under the rim.

Place a small heatproof plate or trivet in the bottom of a large, deep saucepan and stand the pudding basin on it.

Continued overleaf

Multi-plant Puds and Treats

Pour in enough boiling water to come halfway up the sides of the basin. Cover the pan with a tight-fitting lid and bring the water to a simmer over a medium-low heat.

Steam the pudding like this for 2 hours, topping up the boiling water a couple of times, as necessary.

Using oven gloves or a tea towel, lift the pudding basin out of the pan and remove the foil or paper. Run a knife around the side of the pudding to loosen it then invert a serving plate over the basin. Now turn the plate and basin over to unmould the pudding onto the plate.

Cut the pudding into slices and serve, with a spoonful of cream, yoghurt or crème fraîche, or my sunflower and oat cream.

Swaps

Of course you can play around with the dried fruit here, swapping in all kinds, such as dried cherries or cranberries, and dried apples or pears, chopped up to the size of large raisins. I've done just this, and added some festive spice too, to give you...

...A Lighter Christmas Pud

Add 2 tsp ground mixed spice to the dry flour and ground almond mix. Add 50g dried cherries or cranberries and 50g chopped dried apples or pears to the rest of the dried fruit (for a fruitier pud – it is Christmas!) You can stick to the lemony ginger topping as above, or customise with some festive booze – replace the lemon juice with 75ml rum, brandy or whisky, and add the grated zest of an orange plus a generous squeeze of the juice.

Tutti-frutti Semifreddo

Even yummy ice creams can get the 'more plants please' makeover. Ripe bananas are a great way to sweeten them, and work particularly well for this take on the classic tutti-frutti ice cream. Soaking the dried fruits in citrus juice makes them tangy and luscious, and the zest is a nice bonus of colour and flavour.

Serves 6–8

1 large orange
2 limes or 1 lemon
50g raisins
50g dried apricots (unsulphured), chopped into 5 or 6 pieces
50g dried cherries
4 very ripe bananas (about 350g peeled weight)
300g natural whole-milk yoghurt
200g crème fraîche

To serve (optional)
Toasted nuts (hazelnuts or almonds) and/or pumpkin seeds, roughly chopped and mixed with a pinch of salt

Line a 1 litre loaf tin with baking paper (or use a similar glass loaf dish, unlined.)

Pare or grate the zest from the orange and limes or lemon, being careful not to take too much pith. If pared, cut into smaller shards. Place the citrus zest in a small bowl with all the dried fruits.

Squeeze the juice from the citrus fruits and pour it over the dried fruits and zest. Leave for at least 3 hours, ideally overnight, to allow the fruits to absorb the juice and plump up.

Place the peeled bananas in a food processor or blender with the yoghurt and crème fraîche and blitz until smooth. Scrape into a large bowl and place in the freezer.

After about 1½ hours, take out the bowl and whisk the frozen edges back into the middle. Repeat an hour or so later, this time finishing by stirring in the dried fruit, citrus zest and any remaining soaking liquor.

Pack the mixture into the lined tin or dish and place in the freezer for at least 4–5 hours to freeze completely. You can now keep it frozen for up to 3 months.

To serve, remove from the freezer and allow to sit for 20 minutes or so. Wrap a warm wet cloth around the outside of the container to help release the semifreddo, then turn it out onto a board or large plate, peeling away the paper as you do so.

Slice the semifreddo and serve at once, sprinkling over a few toasted nuts and/or seeds if you like.

Rum and Raisin Semifreddo
For a boozy version, simply replace the limes or lemon with 100ml rum. Add to the orange juice for soaking the fruit.

Very Berry Ripple Fro-yo

This is a lovely, lighter alternative to a fruity ice cream – quick and easy to put together. And you can make a dairy-free version by using my Sunflower and oat cream in place of the crème fraîche.

8–10 servings

600g mixed strawberries, raspberries and blueberries (about 200g of each, but varying that is fine), plus extra to serve (optional)
200g natural whole-milk yoghurt (or plant-based yoghurt)
200g crème fraîche (or Sunflower and oat cream, page 220)
75g caster sugar

In a food processor, blitz 400g of the berries with the yoghurt, crème fraîche and 50g of the sugar until smooth and creamy. Pour into a large bowl and place this in the freezer.

In a small bowl, roughly mash the remaining 200g berries and mix with the rest of the sugar to get a nice purée; set aside for the ripple.

After about 1½ hours, take out the bowl and whisk the frozen edges back into the middle. Repeat an hour or so later, this time finishing by rippling through the crushed berries – swirl the berry purée through the mix to get some nice streaks and ripples.

Now pack the mixture into a small freezerproof container and place in the freezer for at least 4–5 hours to freeze completely. You can now keep it frozen for up to 3 months.

To serve, remove from the freezer and allow to sit for 15 minutes or so, to soften slightly. Scoop the fro-yo into bowls and serve, with more of the same berries (some whole, some crushed) if you like.

Peach and Berry Ripple Fro-yo

Peel, halve and stone 600g very ripe peaches or nectarines. Roughly chop and then blitz as above. For the ripple, crush 200g raspberries and/or strawberries with the sugar. Continue and freeze as above.

Fro-yo Lollies

The same mixture makes lovely lollies which kids (and adults too!) will love. Don't worry about the ripple for this mix, just blitz all the fruit and sugar with the yoghurt, then pour into lolly moulds, and freeze.

Beetroot and Chocolate Torte

This fantastic vegan tart has been a favourite at River Cottage for several years now. The beetroot is not just a gesture, but an integral part of the dish, adding to the torte's texture, colour, flavour and natural sweetness.

Admittedly, 350g is quite a hefty dose of dark chocolate, but this is intended to be a very luxurious pud! Plus, there is no added sugar, and the chocolate does the all-important the job of setting the torte as it cools.

The seedy nut crust, flavoured with cocoa, is also a delight.

Serves 8–10

Seedy nut crust
50g coconut oil, plus a little extra
  to grease the tin
180g hazelnuts
50g pumpkin or sunflower seeds
  (or a mix)
50g golden syrup
15g cocoa powder
A pinch of fine sea salt

Filling
320g raw beetroot, peeled
100ml almond milk
350g dark chocolate (minimum
  70% cocoa solids) buttons, or
  chopped
40ml brandy (optional)
A pinch of fine sea salt

To serve
Sunflower and oat cream (page
  220), or cream, ice cream or
  crème fraîche for a non-vegan
  option
Strawberries or other berries
  (optional)

Preheat the oven to 190°C/Fan 170°C/Gas 5. Lightly grease a 20cm tart tin, 3.5–4cm deep (with a removable base) with a little coconut oil.

To make the seedy nut crust, spread the hazelnuts and pumpkin and/or sunflower seeds out on a baking tray and toast in the oven for 5–6 minutes. Remove from the oven and leave to cool for a few moments then tip the seed and nut mix into a small food processor and blitz to a rough textured crumb (coarser than ground almonds, more like instant coffee granules). Set aside.

Melt the coconut oil in a small saucepan over a low heat and then add the golden syrup, cocoa powder and salt. Stir it all together until melted and smoothly combined then take the pan off the heat.

Stir the ground seed and nut mix into the warm melted mixture until evenly combined and then set aside to cool down completely.

Once cooled, tip the seedy nut mix into the tart tin and press it firmly and evenly onto the base and right up the sides of the tin, using your fingertips, to form a case for the filling. Place the tart case in the fridge to firm up while you make the filling.

For the filling, cut the beetroot onto cubes, place in a saucepan and pour on enough cold water to cover. Bring to the boil, lower the heat and simmer for about 30 minutes until tender.

Once cooked, drain the beetroot thoroughly and measure 250g; place this in a jug blender and add the almond milk. Blitz to a smooth purée.

Melt the dark chocolate in a heatproof bowl over a pan of gently simmering water, making sure the base of the bowl isn't touching the water. Stir until silky smooth then remove from the heat. Now gently, but thoroughly, fold in the beetroot purée, brandy if using, and sea salt.

Continued overleaf

Take the tart tin from the fridge and carefully pour the filling into the seedy nut tart case to fill it completely. Smooth over very lightly with a palette knife. (If there's any filling left, scrape it into a ramekin to enjoy separately.)

Place the torte in the fridge to chill for at least 2 hours, until the filling is fully set.

To serve, take the torte from the fridge and wrap a warm damp cloth around the outside of the tin for 30 seconds or so to help loosen the crust. Carefully release the torte from the tin and transfer to a serving plate.

Cut the torte into slices and serve with sunflower and oat cream, or cream, ice cream or crème fraîche, and fresh berries if they are in season.

Swaps

You can make this lovely torte with cooked squash, celeriac or parsnips, instead of the beetroot – each gives a different flavour but all are delicious. Also, you can use ground flax seeds in the crust instead of pumpkin/ sunflower seeds, adding them to the blitzed toasted nuts.
If you don't wish to keep the pud vegan, you can use butter instead of coconut oil in the crust.

Hob-nobby Shortcrust Pastry

I developed this pastry to go with the frangipane tart overleaf, but I wanted to give you a separate recipe, as it really is a great all-rounder. The oats and ground almonds give it a lovely hob-nobby texture, and poppy seeds lend an appealing speckled finish. You can swap this pastry into any recipe that uses a shortcrust pastry case; just leave out the sugar for savoury recipes.

**Makes enough to line
a 24cm tart tin**

120g fine plain wholemeal flour
100g plain white flour, plus extra
  to dust
50g porridge oats
20g golden caster sugar
  (optional, omit for a savoury tart)
30g poppy seeds or ground flax
  seeds (optional)
A pinch of salt
125g chilled butter, diced or
  coarsely grated
1 medium egg, beaten

Combine the two flours, oats, sugar (for a sweet pastry), poppy seeds if using, and the salt in a large bowl, or the bowl of a food processor. Add the butter and either rub in with your fingertips, or pulse in the processor, until the mixture resembles fine crumbs.

Add the beaten egg gradually – either to the bowl, working it in with a table knife, or trickling it into the processor with the motor running. Add a little cold water too, just enough to bring the pastry together into large clumps; don't overwork it.

Tip the pastry onto a floured surface and use your hands to bring it together, then knead it briefly into a ball. Flatten it into a thick disc, then wrap and chill in the fridge for at least 30 minutes, ideally 1–2 hours, before using. It will keep for 48 hours.

Nutty Seedy Frangipane Tart

This is a lovely variation of the classic almond tart I've been making for decades, and it's my new go-to version. Made with at least two varieties each of nuts and seeds and attractively speckled with poppy seeds, it looks and tastes delicious. The Hob-nobby pastry case is nice and crispy and you can make and bake it a day ahead of filling if that's more convenient. Once cooled, the tart will keep in a cake tin for a day or two.

Let the season determine which fruits to serve alongside. Fresh berries and cherries are lovely in the summer, stewed plums in the autumn, and either of the compotes on page 34 would be great in autumn and winter. The fruits suggested for the crumble on pages 234 and 237 would also work well.

Serves 8

1 quantity Hob-nobby shortcrust pastry, page 250

Seedy frangipane filling

100g almonds, hazelnuts or pistachios (or a mix)

100g pumpkin or sunflower seeds (or a mix)

200g unsalted butter, softened

80g golden caster sugar

3 medium eggs (at room temperature), beaten

2 tbsp plain flour

30g poppy seeds

Topping

25g extra pumpkin seeds or flaked almonds

To serve

Seasonal fruit compote or fresh berries or pitted fresh cherries (see above)

Yoghurt or crème fraîche (optional)

Preheat the oven to 180°C/160°C Fan/Gas 4.

Roll out the shortcrust pastry on a floured surface, as thinly as you comfortably can, turning it once or twice and dusting with a little more flour. Use it to line a 24cm loose-based fluted tart tin, pressing the pastry into the corners and trimming away the excess overhanging the rim of the tin.

Place the tart tin on a baking tray. Prick the pastry base in a few places with a fork. Line the pastry case with baking paper, then add a layer of baking beans or dried beans or rice. Bake in the oven for 15 minutes, then remove the paper and beans and return the pastry case to the oven for 5–10 minutes until it looks dry and cooked and is just starting to colour in places. Leave the pastry case to cool a little.

For the filling, tip the nuts and pumpkin/sunflower seeds onto a large baking sheet, spread them out and toast in the oven for 8–10 minutes, until fragrant and starting to turn golden, stirring once halfway through to ensure even colouring. Take out the tray and lower the oven setting to 170°C/150°C Fan/Gas 3.

Tip the toasted nuts and seeds into a bowl and leave to cool for at least 10 minutes. Once cooled, transfer them to a food processor and blitz until the mix is the texture of ground almonds – don't overdo it or you'll end up with a nut butter!

Using a free-standing mixer, or an electric hand whisk and bowl, beat the softened butter and sugar together until light and fluffy. Now whisk in the beaten egg, a little at time, adding a shake of flour with each addition. Once half of the egg is incorporated, stop the mixer and scrape down the sides of the bowl with a spatula, then continue. Finally, mix in the blitzed nutty seed mixture and the poppy seeds, until just incorporated.

Continued overleaf

Spoon the frangipane into the baked tart case, spreading it evenly. Sprinkle a few whole pumpkin seeds or flaked almonds evenly over the surface and bake for 30 minutes.

Turn the oven setting up to 200°C/180°C Fan/Gas 6 and cook for another 10–15 minutes until the frangipane is firm and golden brown on top.

Remove from the oven and place the tart tin on a wire rack. Leave to cool for at least 15 minutes before removing from the tin.

Serve the tart at room temperature, cut into slices, with a fruit compote or fresh berries or cherries alongside, plus a dollop of yoghurt or crème fraîche if you like.

Swaps and Additions

Instead of serving fruit on the side, you can bake it into the tart. This works best with fairly firm fruits that don't give off too much water, such as pears, or dried fruit, as follows:

Pear Frangipane Tart

Peel 4–5 pears and cut them lengthways into quarters, slicing out the core. Arrange them in the baked pastry case, thinner ends pointing to the middle, then spread over the frangipane and bake as above.

Apricot or Prune Frangipane Tart

Soak 150g dried apricots (unsulphured) or pitted prunes in 300ml tea, orange juice or kombucha for at least 3 hours, or overnight, before you make the tart. Drain the fruit (keeping the soaking liquor as a chef's perk, it's delicious) then fold the fruit into the frangipane mix just before filling the pastry case. Bake as above.

Courgette, Honey and Lemon Cake

The mighty lemon drizzle cake is everyone's favourite bake. This spin on it has the unlikely inclusion of courgettes, which balances the sweetness and keeps the cake nice and moist too. It's also a great way to make a dent in a glut of summer courgettes. The lemon drizzle topping makes it irresistibly zingy. You can also serve the cake as a dessert with crème fraîche, summer berries and an extra trickle of honey.

Makes 8–10 slices

350g coarsely grated courgettes
  (about 2 medium)
½ tsp fine salt
150g wholemeal spelt flour
100g fine plain wholemeal flour
100g ground almonds or
  hazelnuts
½ tsp bicarbonate soda
1 tsp baking powder
30g poppy seeds (optional)
125ml rapeseed or coconut oil
50g soft light brown sugar
30g honey
3 medium eggs
Finely grated zest and juice of
  2 lemons
4 sprigs of thyme, leaves picked
  and chopped (optional)
50ml milk

Lemon drizzle
Finely grated zest and juice of
  1 lemon
1 tbsp honey
20g caster sugar

Preheat the oven to 180°C/160°C Fan/Gas 4 and line a 1kg (2lb) loaf tin with baking paper.

Tip the grated courgettes into a fine-meshed sieve set over a bowl. Sprinkle with the salt and toss through (it will draw out moisture from the veg). Leave to drain for 20 minutes or so, then press the courgettes with the back of a spoon to get rid of a bit more water.

In a bowl, mix together the flours, ground nuts, bicarbonate of soda, baking powder and poppy seeds if using. Set aside.

In a large bowl, whisk together the oil, sugar and honey. Beat in the eggs, one by one, then stir in the grated courgettes, lemon zest and juice, and the thyme if using. Now gently fold in the flour mixture, alternately with the milk. Pour the mixture into the prepared loaf tin and bake for 45–50 minutes until golden and risen.

While the cake is in the oven, make the lemon drizzle. In a small bowl, lightly mix the lemon zest and juice with the honey and sugar to combine without dissolving the sugar.

To check the cake is cooked, insert a skewer into the middle – it should come out clean. As soon as you take the cake from the oven, spoon the lemon drizzle over the surface. Leave the cake in the tin for 10 minutes then transfer it to a wire rack and allow to cool completely before slicing and serving.

Swaps and Additions
Use grated squash or pumpkin instead of courgette. Or go 50:50 with courgette and a grated root, such as beetroot, carrot or parsnip. Just mix it with the courgette before salting. Beetroot, as you can imagine, makes a gorgeous pinky purple version.

Maple and Nut Butter Flapjacks

I'm a big flapjack fan, and my approach to this enduring family favourite is always evolving. As you can imagine, this is my plantiest flapjack yet. Of course the mix of dried fruit, nuts and seeds can be varied as you like, and it's pretty much the more (varieties) the merrier. And you can use any nut butter, but my nut and seed butter on page 213 is especially good!

Makes 10–12

200g porridge oats
100g seeds, such as sunflower
  or pumpkin (or a mix)
1 tsp caraway or fennel seeds
  (optional)
50g dried apricots (unsulphured),
  or dried apple or pear, chopped
50g sultanas or raisins
50g nuts, such as hazelnuts,
  walnuts, almonds or macadamia
  nuts, roughly chopped
150g organic peanut butter,
  Nut and seed butter (page 213)
  or other nut butter
30g soft light brown sugar
3–4 tbsp coconut or olive oil
  (or melted unsalted butter)
2 tbsp maple syrup (or honey)

Preheat the oven to 200°C/180°C Fan/Gas 6. Line a 20cm square baking tin with baking paper.

Mix the oats, seeds, spice seeds if using, dried fruit and chopped nuts together in a large bowl.

Put the nut butter, sugar, 3 tbsp oil (or butter) and maple syrup (or honey) into a saucepan, place over a low heat and stir gently until everything is melted and well blended. Pour onto the oat mixture and stir well to combine. If the mixture doesn't quite come together mix in another 1 tbsp oil (or melted butter).

Tip the flapjack mixture into the prepared tin, spread out and press down with the back of a spoon into an even layer. Bake in the oven for 20–25 minutes until lightly golden (and a little darker at the edges). Remove from the oven and leave to cool in the tin.

Once cooled, cut the flapjack sheet into 10 or 12 slices. These will keep in an airtight container for up to a week.

Chocolate and Spice Cookies

There's no reason why delicious treats like cookies can't help you rack up your plant count with some healthy seeds and lovely spices – and chocolate! I love the specific combination of ginger and cardamom with chocolate, but you can use a teaspoonful of mixed spice if that's more convenient.

You can start with fridge-cold butter (as it will be melted), so it is easy to knock these up at short notice. This is a fairly small batch – just double up the quantities if you would like to make more. Below are some lovely variations to this simple recipe.

Makes 12

125g butter
40g soft light brown sugar
2 cardamom pods (or ½ tsp ground cardamom)
125g fine plain wholemeal flour
75g porridge oats
50g sunflower or pumpkin seeds (or a mix)
1 tsp ground ginger
70g dark chocolate (70% cocoa solids), chopped into small (pea-sized) pieces

Preheat the oven to 180°C/160°C Fan/Gas 4. Line a baking sheet with baking paper.

Melt the butter and sugar together in a small saucepan over a low heat, stirring often until well blended. Take off the heat and leave to cool a little.

In the meantime, if using cardamom pods, bash the pods with a rolling pin to release the seeds then use a pestle and mortar to crush these. Discard the broken pods and use the crushed seeds.

Mix the flour, oats, seeds, ground ginger and cardamom together and stir into the melted mixture until evenly blended. If the mixture is still warm, leave it to cool for a few more minutes before adding the chocolate (so the pieces don't melt). Stir to distribute the chocolate through the cookie batter.

Take dessertspoonfuls of the mixture and place on the lined baking sheet, leaving a 3–4cm space in between as they will spread a little on baking. Use the back of the spoon to flatten each cookie into a rough circle, no more than 1cm deep. (I aim for 12 fairly small cookies.)

Bake in the oven for 12–15 minutes, depending on size, until the cookies are turning golden, and are more deeply coloured at the edges. They'll still be a bit soft at this point: leave to cool completely and crisp up before removing from the tray.

You can store the cookies in an airtight container for up to a week – good luck with keeping them that long!

Swaps
Try adding raisins, chopped dried apricots (unsulphured) or other dried fruit: up to 50g can be stirred in with, or instead of, the chocolate.
For nutty chocolate cookies, use roughly chopped hazelnuts, peanuts, cashews, walnuts or almonds instead of the sunflower or pumpkin seeds.
You can use 1 tsp ground mixed spice instead of cardamom and ginger.

Index

264   Index

Acknowledgements

No cookbook comes together without a dedicated team working behind the scenes, and there are many talented people I want to thank.

Firstly, I want to express my gratitude to Professor Tim Spector OBE, who graciously agreed to write an introduction to this book, outlining the science behind the concept of eating 30 plants a week. He has done so brilliantly and clearly.

Tim's colleague at ZOE, medical scientist and nutritionist Dr Federica Amati, also read the text closely and made some very helpful suggestions. My sincere thanks to her.

Thanks to photographer Lizzie Mayson who has done an amazing job of capturing these dishes in all their multi-plant glory. Lizzie was helped throughout by her assistant Abby Fisk. Sincere thanks to them both for their professionalism and positivity.

I am also incredibly grateful to designer Luke Bird for his fantastic work and delightful graphics. He has taken my raw copy and presented it with great elan: this book would look much less impressive and less persuasive without his touch.

For her superb input in recipe development, as well as rigorous testing and outstanding styling on the photo shoots, huge thanks go to Kitty Coles. A delectable chunk of recipe ideas for the book also came from the creative kitchen of Lulu Cox, to whom further heartfelt thanks.

We were skilfully assisted on the shoots by Clare Cole, El Kemp and Lucy Cottle, who cooked the dishes we photographed with flair and relish. And thanks also to my long-term collaborator Gill Meller for invaluable help bringing in the final photo shoot.

River Cottage Culinary Director Gelf Alderson, Head Chef Connor Reed and Chef Tutor Chiara Tomasoni have all offered up some completely delicious creations of theirs from recent River Cottage menus, while Rachel de Thample, who leads our fermenting courses at River Cottage, inspired me with her suggestions for pickles and ferments. I am truly grateful to you all. And for his constant support on this, and all my other projects, massive thanks to my River Cottage partner Stewart Dodd.

Janet Illsley has been, as ever, a brilliant and eagle-eyed project manager, guiding me through the various stages before the book went to press, keeping us all on schedule and making sure the text was absolutely ship-shape and watertight. And to proofreader Sally Somers, thank you for taking a fine-tooth comb to each and every word: it is detailed work that is sometimes overlooked, but vital.

Antony Topping, my agent, has been my trusted ally and friend, providing honest and thoughtful feedback, for almost 30 years now. I'd be lost without him. Holly Faulks, Antony's colleague at Greene & Heaton, has also been hugely helpful from start to finish.

I am fast approaching the end of a second decade of collaboration with my publishers, Bloomsbury, and I want to thank them for their unwavering support. Some of the personnel has changed over the years, but my gratitude has not. Huge thanks first to Laura Brodie for her superb production skills, Akua Boateng for fly-on-the-wall fun on social media, and to Isobel Turton and Ellen Williams for making publicity always so smooth and focused. Em North has offered astute editorial guidance throughout the making of this book, and my editor, Rowan Yapp, has been a wholehearted and active supporter of the project from the moment it was first mooted. Thank you all.

As many of the above could tell you, I couldn't really function without Jess Upton, my endlessly efficient PA, who knows exactly where I'm meant to be and what I'm meant to be doing at all times, and conveys that information to all who need it with unstinting grace and consideration.

And to my family, Marie, Chloe, Oscar, Freddie and Louisa, my heartfelt thanks for your untiring love and support, and for being always – metaphorically when not actually physically – at our table.

BLOOMSBURY PUBLISHING
Bloomsbury Publishing Plc
50 Bedford Square, London, WC1B 3DP, UK
29 Earlsfort Terrace, Dublin 2, Ireland
BLOOMSBURY, BLOOMSBURY PUBLISHING and the Diana logo are
trademarks of Bloomsbury Publishing Plc

First published in Great Britain 2024
Text © Hugh Fearnley-Whittingstall 2024
Photographs © Lizzie Mayson 2024
except those on page 11 © Jonathan Ring and page 48 © Hugh Fearnley-Whittingstall
Cover photograph © Jonathan Ring 2024
Illustrations © Shutterstock 2024

A catalogue record for this book is available from the British Library
Library of Congress Cataloguing-in-Publication data has been applied for

ISBN: HB: 978-1-5266-7252-0; ePUB: 978-1-5266-7253-7; ePDF: 978-1-5266-7254-4

10 9 8 7 6 5 4 3 2 1

Project Editor: Janet Illsley
Designer: Luke Bird
Photographer: Lizzie Mayson
Photographer's Assistant: Abbie Fisk
Food and Props Stylist: Kitty Coles
Additional Food Stylist: Gill Meller
Assistant Food Stylists: Clare Cole, Lucy Cottle and El Kemp
Indexer: Hilary Bird

Printed and bound in China by RR Donnelley Asia Printing Solutions Ltd

To find out more about our authors and books visit www.bloomsbury.com
and sign up for our newsletters

18 Everyday Fruit Bowl

Apples ☐ ☐ ☐ ☐ ☐
Pears ☐ ☐ ☐ ☐ ☐
Plums ☐ ☐ ☐ ☐ ☐
Bananas/Plantains ☐ ☐ ☐ ☐ ☐
Grapes ☐ ☐ ☐ ☐ ☐
Cherries ☐ ☐ ☐ ☐ ☐
.... ☐ ☐ ☐ ☐ ☐

19 Citrus Fruits

Lemons ☐ ☐ ☐ ☐ ☐
Oranges ☐ ☐ ☐ ☐ ☐
Clementines, Easy Peelers etc ☐ ☐ ☐ ☐ ☐
Limes ☐ ☐ ☐ ☐ ☐
Grapefruit ☐ ☐ ☐ ☐ ☐
.... ☐ ☐ ☐ ☐ ☐

20 Summer Berries

Strawberries ☐ ☐ ☐ ☐ ☐
Raspberries ☐ ☐ ☐ ☐ ☐
Blueberries ☐ ☐ ☐ ☐ ☐
Blackberries ☐ ☐ ☐ ☐ ☐
Blackcurrants/Redcurrants ☐ ☐ ☐ ☐ ☐
Gooseberries ☐ ☐ ☐ ☐ ☐
.... ☐ ☐ ☐ ☐ ☐
Rhubarb *(honorary fruit!)* ☐ ☐ ☐ ☐ ☐

21 Mediterranean/ Exotic Fruit Bowl

Peaches ☐ ☐ ☐ ☐ ☐
Nectarines ☐ ☐ ☐ ☐ ☐
Melon ☐ ☐ ☐ ☐ ☐
Watermelon ☐ ☐ ☐ ☐ ☐
Apricots ☐ ☐ ☐ ☐ ☐
Figs ☐ ☐ ☐ ☐ ☐
Kiwi Fruit ☐ ☐ ☐ ☐ ☐
Mango ☐ ☐ ☐ ☐ ☐
Pomegranate ☐ ☐ ☐ ☐ ☐
Papaya ☐ ☐ ☐ ☐ ☐
Passion Fruit ☐ ☐ ☐ ☐ ☐
Pineapple ☐ ☐ ☐ ☐ ☐
.... ☐ ☐ ☐ ☐ ☐

22 Dried Fruits

Raisins ☐ ☐ ☐ ☐ ☐
Sultanas ☐ ☐ ☐ ☐ ☐
Dried Apricots ☐ ☐ ☐ ☐ ☐
Prunes ☐ ☐ ☐ ☐ ☐
Dried Apple ☐ ☐ ☐ ☐ ☐
Dried Pear ☐ ☐ ☐ ☐ ☐
Dates ☐ ☐ ☐ ☐ ☐
Dried Figs ☐ ☐ ☐ ☐ ☐
Cranberries ☐ ☐ ☐ ☐ ☐
.... ☐ ☐ ☐ ☐ ☐
.... ☐ ☐ ☐ ☐ ☐

23 Nuts

Peanuts ☐ ☐ ☐ ☐ ☐
Hazelnuts ☐ ☐ ☐ ☐ ☐
Walnuts ☐ ☐ ☐ ☐ ☐
Almonds ☐ ☐ ☐ ☐ ☐
Pecans ☐ ☐ ☐ ☐ ☐
Brazil Nuts ☐ ☐ ☐ ☐ ☐
Pine Nuts ☐ ☐ ☐ ☐ ☐
Cashews ☐ ☐ ☐ ☐ ☐
Chestnuts ☐ ☐ ☐ ☐ ☐
Pistachios ☐ ☐ ☐ ☐ ☐
.... ☐ ☐ ☐ ☐ ☐
.... ☐ ☐ ☐ ☐ ☐

24 Tinned Pulses

Butter Beans ☐ ☐ ☐ ☐ ☐
Chickpeas ☐ ☐ ☐ ☐ ☐
Cannellini Beans ☐ ☐ ☐ ☐ ☐
Flageolet Beans ☐ ☐ ☐ ☐ ☐
Black Beans ☐ ☐ ☐ ☐ ☐
Red Kidney Beans ☐ ☐ ☐ ☐ ☐
Borlotti Beans ☐ ☐ ☐ ☐ ☐
Pinto Beans ☐ ☐ ☐ ☐ ☐
Carlin Peas ☐ ☐ ☐ ☐ ☐
Black-eyed Beans ☐ ☐ ☐ ☐ ☐
Mung Beans ☐ ☐ ☐ ☐ ☐
Aduki Beans ☐ ☐ ☐ ☐ ☐
.... ☐ ☐ ☐ ☐ ☐
.... ☐ ☐ ☐ ☐ ☐